First World War
and Army of Occupation
War Diary
France, Belgium and Germany

21 DIVISION
Divisional Troops
98 Field Company Royal Engineers
11 September 1915 - 7 June 1919

WO95/2144/2

The Naval & Military Press Ltd
www.nmarchive.com
Published in association with The National Archives

Published by

The Naval & Military Press Ltd

Unit 10 Ridgewood Industrial Park,

Uckfield, East Sussex,

TN22 5QE England

Tel: +44 (0) 1825 749494

www.naval-military-press.com

www.nmarchive.com

This diary has been reprinted in facsimile from the original. Any imperfections are inevitably reproduced and the quality may fall short of modern type and cartographic standards.

© Crown Copyright
Images reproduced by permission of The National Archives, London, England, 2015.

Contents

Document type	Place/Title	Date From	Date To
Heading	WO95/2144/2 98 Field Company Royal Experience		
Heading	21st Division 98th Field Coy R.E. Sep 1915-Jun 1919		
Heading	21st Division 98th F.C.R.E. Vol I Sep 1-15		
War Diary	Havre	11/09/1915	12/09/1915
War Diary	Stomer	13/09/1915	13/09/1915
War Diary	Mentque	14/09/1915	19/09/1915
War Diary	On The March	20/09/1915	23/09/1915
War Diary	Fosse 7 De Bethune	24/09/1915	25/09/1915
War Diary	Near By	26/09/1915	26/09/1915
War Diary	Noyelles	27/09/1915	28/09/1915
War Diary	On The March	29/09/1915	30/09/1915
Heading	21st Division 98th F.C.R.E. Vol 2 Oct 15		
War Diary	Steenbecque	01/10/1915	01/10/1915
War Diary	Pradelles	02/10/1915	10/10/1915
War Diary	Courterue	11/10/1915	17/10/1915
War Diary	Armentieres	18/10/1915	31/10/1915
Heading	21st Division 98th F.C.R.E. Vol 3 Nov 15		
War Diary	Armentieres	01/11/1915	30/11/1915
Heading	21st Div 98th F.C.R.E. Vol 4		
War Diary	Armentieres	01/12/1915	31/12/1915
Heading	21st Divisional Engineers 98th Field Company R.E. January 1916		
Heading	21st D 98th F.C.R.E. Vol 5 Jan 16		
Heading	War Diary Of 98th Field Co. R.E. From Jan 1st-Jan 31st 1916 Volume 5		
War Diary	Armentieres	01/01/1916	31/01/1916
Heading	21st Divisional Engineers 98th Field Company R.E. February 1916		
Heading	War Diary Of 98th Field Company R.E. From Feb 1st-29th 1916 Volume VI		
War Diary	Armentieres	01/02/1916	29/02/1916
War Diary		18/02/1916	24/02/1916
War Diary		01/02/1916	27/02/1916
Heading	21st Divisional Engineers 98th Field Company R.E. March 1916		
Heading	War Diary Of 98th Field Company R.E. From March 1st-31st 1916 Volume VII		
War Diary	Armentieres	01/03/1916	31/03/1916
Heading	21st Divisional Engineers 98th Field Company R.E. April 1916		
War Diary	Bailleul	01/04/1916	01/04/1916
War Diary	Allonville	02/04/1916	06/04/1916
War Diary	Buire Sur L'ancre	07/04/1916	30/04/1916
Heading	21st Divisional Engineers 98th Field Company R.E. May 1916		
Heading	War Diary Of 98th Field Co R.E. From May 1st-31st 1916 Vol IX		
War Diary	Buire	01/05/1916	28/05/1916
Heading	21st Divisional Engineers 98th Field Company R.E. June 1916		

Heading	War Diary Of 98th Field Co R.E. From June 1st-30th 1916 Volume X		
Heading	DAG 3rd Echelon	30/06/1916	30/06/1916
War Diary	Buire-Sur-Ancre	01/06/1916	30/06/1916
Heading	21st Divisional Engineers 98th Field Company R.E. July 1916		
Heading	War Diary Of 98th Field Co RE. 21st Division From July 1st-31st 1916 Volume XI		
War Diary	Becourt Valley	01/07/1916	03/07/1916
War Diary	Map 1/10,000 Sheet 17 (Amiens)	04/07/1916	04/07/1916
War Diary	Fremont	05/07/1916	07/07/1916
War Diary	Hangest	08/07/1916	10/07/1916
War Diary	Ville-Sous-Corbie	11/07/1916	12/07/1916
War Diary	Becourt Valley	13/07/1916	14/07/1916
War Diary	Near Fricourt	15/07/1916	17/07/1916
War Diary	Ville-Sous Corbie	18/07/1916	19/07/1916
War Diary	Allonville	20/07/1916	22/07/1916
War Diary	Monts En Ternois	23/07/1916	24/07/1916
War Diary	Blavincourt	25/07/1916	28/07/1916
War Diary	Arras	29/07/1916	31/07/1916
Heading	21st Divisional Engineers 98th Field Company R.E. August 1916		
Heading	War Diary Of 98th Field Co R.E. From Aug 1st-31st 1916 Volume XII		
War Diary	Arras	01/08/1916	31/08/1916
Heading	21st Divisional Engineers 98th Field Company R.E. September 1916		
Heading	War Diary Of 98th Field Co R.E. Sept 1st-30th 1916 Volume XIII		
War Diary	Arras	02/09/1916	04/09/1916
War Diary	Noyellette	05/09/1916	05/09/1916
War Diary	Blavincourt	06/09/1916	12/09/1916
War Diary	Famechon	13/09/1916	13/09/1916
War Diary	Dernancourt	14/09/1916	15/09/1916
War Diary	Fricourt Camp	16/09/1916	16/09/1916
War Diary	1 Mile N Of Carnoy	17/09/1916	21/09/1916
War Diary	Bernafay Wood	22/09/1916	30/09/1916
Heading	21st Divisional Engineers 98th Field Company R.E. October 1916		
War Diary	Bernafay Wood	01/10/1916	02/10/1916
War Diary	Dernancourt	03/10/1916	04/10/1916
War Diary	Pont Remy	05/10/1916	08/10/1916
War Diary	Verquigneul	09/10/1916	10/10/1916
War Diary	Noyelles	11/10/1916	31/10/1916
Heading	21st Divisional Engineers 98th Field Company R.E. November 1916		
Heading	War Diary Of 98th Field Company R.E. From 1st Nov 1916 To 30th Nov 1916 Vol 15		
War Diary	Noyelles-Lez-Vermelles	08/11/1916	30/11/1916
War Diary	Noyelles	25/11/1916	27/11/1916
Heading	21st Divisional Engineers 98th Field Company R.E. December 1916		
Heading	War Diary Of 98th Field Coy RE From 1st Decr. 1916 To 30th Decr 1916 Vol 16		
War Diary	Noyelles	01/12/1916	30/12/1916

Heading	War Diary Of 98th Field Company R.E. From Janry 2nd 1917 To Janry 31st 1917 Vol 17		
War Diary	Raimbert	02/01/1917	28/01/1917
War Diary	Winnezele J.11.a.6.9 (Sheet 27)	28/01/1917	31/01/1917
Heading	War Diary Of 98th Field Co R.E. 21st Division From Feb 1st-28th 1917 Vol XVIII		
War Diary	Winnezeele	31/01/1917	13/02/1917
War Diary	Bethune	14/02/1917	14/02/1917
War Diary	Noyelles-Lez-Vermelles	15/02/1917	28/02/1917
Heading	War Diary Of 98th Field Co R.E. March 1st-31st 1917 Vol XIX		
War Diary	Noyelles-Lez-Vermelles	01/03/1917	29/03/1917
War Diary	Pommier	30/03/1917	04/04/1917
War Diary	Hamelincourt	05/04/1917	14/04/1917
War Diary	Bailleul-Mont	15/04/1917	23/04/1917
War Diary	Boiry-St-Rictrude	24/04/1917	26/04/1917
War Diary	Judas Farm	27/04/1917	30/04/1917
Heading	War Diary Of 98th Field Company RE From 1st May 1917 To 31st May 1917 Volume 21		
War Diary	Judas Farm Near St. Leger	01/05/1917	06/05/1917
War Diary	Judas Farm	07/05/1917	12/05/1917
War Diary	Bienvillers-Au-Bois	13/05/1917	31/05/1917
Heading	War Diary Of 98th Field Coy R.E. From 1st June 1917 To 30th June 1917 Volume 22		
War Diary	Hamelincourt	01/06/1917	20/06/1917
War Diary	Ransart	21/06/1917	30/06/1917
Heading	War Diary Of 98th Field Company R.E. From 1st July 1917 To 31st July 1917 Volume 23		
War Diary	Ransart	01/07/1917	01/07/1917
War Diary	Hamelincourt	02/07/1917	29/07/1917
War Diary	Boiry Becquerelle	28/07/1917	31/07/1917
Heading	War Diary Of 98th Field Co R.E. From 1st August 1917 To 31st August 1917 Volume 24		
War Diary	Boiry Becquerelle	01/08/1917	08/08/1917
War Diary	St Leger	09/08/1917	27/08/1917
War Diary	Fosseux	28/08/1917	31/08/1917
Heading	War Diary Of 98th Field Company R.E. From 1st Sept 1917 To 30th Sept 1917 Vol 25		
War Diary	Fosseux	01/09/1917	30/09/1917
Heading	War Diary Of 98th Field Company R.E. From 1st Oct 1917 To 31st Oct 1917 Volume 26		
War Diary	Zillebeke Lake	01/10/1917	12/10/1917
War Diary	Bdescheppe	13/10/1917	31/10/1917
Heading	War Diary Of 98th Field Coy R.E. From 1st Nov 1917 To 30th Nov 1917 Volume 26		
War Diary	Ridge Wood	01/11/1917	15/11/1917
War Diary	Bossebome	16/11/1917	17/11/1917
War Diary	Doulieu	18/11/1917	19/11/1917
War Diary	Oblinghem	20/11/1917	20/11/1917
War Diary	Coupigny	21/11/1917	24/11/1917
War Diary	Bajus	25/11/1917	30/11/1917
Heading	98th Field Company R.E. From 1st Dec 1917 To 31st Dec 1917 Volume 27		
War Diary	Near Duisans	01/12/1917	01/12/1917
War Diary	Badaume	02/12/1917	05/12/1917
War Diary	Tincourt	05/12/1917	21/12/1917

War Diary	Near Saulcourt	24/12/1917	31/12/1917
Heading	War Diary Of 98th Field Company R.E. From 1st Janry 1918 To 31st Janry 1918 Volume 28		
War Diary	Near Saulcourt E14f.72 Sheet 62c 1/40,000	01/01/1918	31/01/1918
Heading	War Diary Of 98th Field Company R.E. From 1st February 1918 To 28th February 1918 Volume 29		
War Diary	Saulcourt E 14 F 72 Sheet 62c 1/40,000	01/02/1918	28/02/1918
Heading	21st Div. War Diary 98th Field Company R.E. March 1918		
Heading	War Diary Of 98th Field Co R.E. From 1st March 1918 To 31st March 1918 Volume 30		
War Diary	Saulcourt E 14b.7.2 Sheet 62.c	01/03/1918	21/03/1918
War Diary	E 13.d.4.6	21/03/1918	22/03/1918
War Diary	Aizecourt-Le Bas D23.b.1.7 Sheet 62.c	22/03/1918	22/03/1918
War Diary	Aizecourt-Le Bas	22/03/1918	22/03/1918
War Diary	Haut Allaines	23/03/1918	23/03/1918
War Diary	Clery-Sur-Somme	23/03/1918	23/03/1918
War Diary	Curlu	24/03/1918	24/03/1918
War Diary	Suzanne	24/03/1918	24/03/1918
War Diary	Bray	24/03/1918	24/03/1918
War Diary	L.13.c	25/03/1918	25/03/1918
War Diary	Sheet 62.D Chipilly K.34.a2.8	25/03/1918	25/03/1918
War Diary	Basieux	26/03/1918	27/03/1918
War Diary	Behencourt	28/03/1918	29/03/1918
War Diary	Cardonette	30/03/1918	31/03/1918
Heading	21st Divisional Engineers 98th Field Company R.E. April 1918		
Heading	War Diary Of 98th Field Company R.E. From 1st April 1918 To 30th April 1918 Volume 31		
War Diary	Peselhoek	02/04/1918	02/04/1918
War Diary	Locre	03/04/1918	30/04/1918
Heading	War Diary Of 98th Field Company R.E. From 1st May 1918 To 31st May 1918 Volume No 32		
War Diary	Near Busseboom	01/05/1918	01/05/1918
War Diary	Steenvoorde	02/05/1918	02/05/1918
War Diary	Buysscheure	03/05/1918	04/05/1918
War Diary	Anthenay	06/05/1918	08/05/1918
War Diary	Lhery	12/05/1918	12/05/1918
War Diary	Prouilly	13/05/1918	13/05/1918
War Diary	Hermonville	14/05/1918	27/05/1918
War Diary	Branscourt	28/05/1918	28/05/1918
War Diary	Ville En Tardenois	29/05/1918	29/05/1918
War Diary	Marfaux	29/05/1918	29/05/1918
War Diary	Foret D'Epernay	30/05/1918	30/05/1918
War Diary	Etrechy	31/05/1918	31/05/1918
Heading	War Diary Of 98th Field Company R.E. From 1st June 1918 To 30th June 1918 Volume 33		
War Diary	Etrechy (Chalons 750 1/60,000)	01/06/1918	03/06/1918
War Diary	Courgeonnet (Chalons 50 1/80,000)	04/06/1918	09/06/1918
War Diary	Verdey (Areis, 67 1/80,000)	10/06/1918	13/06/1918
War Diary	Connantray (Arcis, 67 1/80,000)	14/06/1918	16/06/1918
War Diary	Busmenard (Dieppe 1/100,000)	16/06/1918	22/06/1918
War Diary	Etocquigny	22/06/1918	24/06/1918
War Diary	Baromesnil	24/06/1918	24/06/1918
War Diary	Dieppe 1/100,000 Baromesnil	25/06/1918	30/06/1918

Heading	War Diary Of 98th Field Coy R.E. From 1st July 1918 To 31st July 1918 Volume 34		
War Diary	Sheet 570 1/40,000	01/07/1918	01/07/1918
War Diary	Beauquesne	02/07/1918	14/07/1918
War Diary	Sheet 570 Beauquesne	15/07/1918	24/07/1918
War Diary	Englebelmer	25/07/1918	25/07/1918
War Diary	Sheet 57D Englebelmer	26/07/1918	31/07/1918
Heading	War Diary Of 98th Field Coy R.E. From 1st August 1918 To 31st August 1918 Volume 35		
War Diary	Sheet 57 D.S.E 1/20,000 Englebelmer P24c.22	01/08/1918	20/08/1918
War Diary	Sheet 57 D.S.E 1/20,000	21/08/1918	29/08/1918
War Diary	Sheet 57c S.W. 1/20,000	30/08/1918	31/08/1918
Heading	War Diary Of 98th Field Coy R.E. From 1st Sept 1918 To 30th Sept 1918 Volume 36		
War Diary	Sheet 57c S.W. 1/20,000 Butte De Wodencourt	01/09/1918	05/09/1918
War Diary	Sheet 57c 1/40,000	06/09/1918	06/09/1918
War Diary	Sheet 57c 1/40,000 Manancourt	07/09/1918	24/09/1918
War Diary	Heudecourt W.8.d.3.4	25/09/1918	29/09/1918
War Diary	Sheet 57c 1/40,000 Heudecourt	29/09/1918	30/09/1918
Heading	War Diary Of 98th Field Coy R.E. From 1st October 1918 To 31st October 1918 Volume 37		
War Diary	Sheet 57c S.E Heudecourt	01/10/1918	05/10/1918
War Diary	Sheet 57c S.E 1/20,000	05/10/1918	05/10/1918
War Diary	R34.d.8.6	06/10/1918	07/10/1918
War Diary	Sheet 57 B S W 1/20,000	08/10/1918	09/10/1918
War Diary	Guillemont	10/10/1918	12/10/1918
War Diary	Walincourt	13/10/1918	15/10/1918
War Diary	Sheet 57B Walincourt	16/10/1918	22/10/1918
War Diary	Audencourt Sheet 57B Sheet 51A Sheet 51	22/10/1918	23/10/1918
War Diary	Neuvilly	23/10/1918	23/10/1918
War Diary	Ovillers	24/10/1918	24/10/1918
War Diary	Sheet 57B Sheet 51A Ovillers	24/10/1918	25/10/1918
War Diary	Neuvilly	26/10/1918	28/10/1918
War Diary	Vendigies-Au-Bois	29/10/1918	31/10/1918
Heading	War Diary Of 98th Field Coy R.E. From 1st Nov 1918 To 30th Nov 1918 Volume 39		
War Diary	Sheets 57B 51A 51	01/11/1918	01/11/1918
War Diary	Vendegies-Au-Bois	01/11/1918	04/11/1918
War Diary	Poix-Du-Nord	05/11/1918	05/11/1918
War Diary	Locquignol	06/11/1918	06/11/1918
War Diary	Sheet 51 La Tete Noire	07/11/1918	11/11/1918
War Diary	Ropsies W16c	12/11/1918	12/11/1918
War Diary	Damousies	13/11/1918	13/11/1918
War Diary	Sheet 52 Causolre M 30	14/11/1918	14/11/1918
War Diary	Sheet 52 Causolre	15/11/1918	16/11/1918
War Diary	Sheet 51 Ferriere-le-Petite	17/11/1918	20/11/1918
War Diary	Berlaimont	21/11/1918	30/11/1918
War Diary	Ref Valenciennes 1/100,000	30/11/1918	30/11/1918
Miscellaneous	A Form Messages And Signals		
Heading	War Diary Of 98th Field Coy R.E. From 1st Decr 1918 To 31st Decr 1918 Volume 39		
Miscellaneous	A Form Messages And Signals		
War Diary	Valenciennes (1/100,000)	01/12/1918	02/12/1918
War Diary	Amiens (1/10,000) Bovelles	03/12/1918	31/12/1918
Miscellaneous	Adjutant Above dead with There	01/02/1919	01/02/1919

Heading	War Diary Of 98th Field Coy R.E. From 1/1/19 To 31/1/19 Vol 40		
War Diary	Amiens 1/100,000 Bovelles	01/01/1919	31/01/1919
Heading	War Diary Of 98th Field Company R.E. From 1st Feb 1919 To 28th Feb 1919 Volume 41		
War Diary	Amiens 1/100,000 Bovelles	01/02/1919	28/02/1919
War Diary		24/02/1919	24/02/1919
War Diary	Amiens 1/100,000 Bovelles	01/03/1919	06/03/1919
War Diary	Oissy	07/03/1919	08/03/1919
War Diary	Amiens 1/100,000 Oissy	09/03/1919	31/03/1919
War Diary	Amiens 1/100,000 Oissy	27/03/1919	31/03/1919
War Diary	Amiens 1/100,000 Bovelles	01/03/1919	06/03/1919
War Diary	Oissy	07/03/1919	08/03/1919
War Diary	Amiens 1/100,000 Oissy	09/03/1919	25/03/1919
Heading	War Diary Of 98th Field Company R.E. From 1st Apr 1919 To 30th Apr 1919 Vol 44		
War Diary	Amiens 1/100,000 Oissy	01/04/1919	04/04/1919
War Diary	Le Catelet	05/04/1919	23/04/1919
War Diary	Amiens 1/100,000 Le Catelet (Somme)	23/04/1919	30/04/1919
Heading	War Diary Of 98th Field Company R.E. From 1st May 1919 To 31st May 1919 Volume 44		
War Diary	Amiens 1/100,000 Le Catelet (Somme)	01/05/1919	31/05/1919
War Diary	Amiens Le Catelet (Somme)	10/05/1919	24/05/1919
Heading	War Diary Of 98th Field Company R.E. From 1st June 1919 To 7th June 1919 Vol 46		
War Diary	Le Catelet (Somme) Amiens 1/100,000	01/06/1919	07/06/1919
Miscellaneous	98th Field Coy R.E.		
Miscellaneous	98th Field Company R.E.		
Miscellaneous			
Miscellaneous	98th Field Company R.E.		

WO95/2144/2
98 Field Company Royal Engineers

21ST DIVISION

98TH FIELD COY R.E.

SEP 1915-JUN 1919

21st Division

121
7/121

98th F.C. R.E.
Vol: I

Sept. 15

June '19

Instructions regarding War Diaries and Intelligence Summaries are contained in F. S. Regs., Part II. and the Staff Manual respectively. Title pages will be prepared in manuscript.

WAR DIARY
or
~~INTELLIGENCE SUMMARY.~~
(Erase heading not required.)

Army Form C. 2118.

Page 1

Place	Date	Hour	Summary of Events and Information	Remarks and references to Appendices
HAVRE	11/9/15		Landed – went to No 5 Rest Camp	
do	12/15		Entrained	
ST OMER	13/15		Detrained, went into billets at MENTQUE	
MENTQUE	14/15		In Billets	
do	15		do	
do	16		–	
do	17		–	
do	18		–	
do	19		–	
On the March	20		Marching to WARDRECQUES	
do	21		do to LA GOULEE	
do	22		do to AUCHEL	
do	23		do to HOUCHIN	
FOSSE 7 de BETHUNE	24	——	do to Fosse No 7 de BETHUNE. Took 2 Sections & cleared way for attack of 63rd INF BDE. Returned and parked wagons. No casualties.	
	25	——	Clearing LENS road of dead and repairing gaps. Went forward as infantry with 126 Co + Inf. details to hold old English front line trench. A little shell fire + gas – no casualties. Relieved by Guards Brigade. Marched to Noyelles at 4 am	
near Ly.	26			
NOYELLES	27	——	At NOYELLES. Preparing water supply for 21st Div	
do	28	——	do do + marched to BETHUNE	
On the march	29	——	BETHUNE to LA TIRMAND near RELY	
	30		LA TIRMANDE to STEENBECQUE	

J. M. [illegible] RE
OC 95 FD CoRE
3/10/15

2353 Wt. W2544/1454 700,000 5/15 D. D. & L. A.D.S.S./Forms/C. 2118.

21st Division

121/7595

98th F.C. R.E.
Vol: 2

Oct 15

Instructions regarding War Diaries and Intelligence Summaries are contained in F. S. Regs., Part II. and the Staff Manual respectively. Title pages will be prepared in manuscript.

WAR DIARY
or
INTELLIGENCE SUMMARY.
(*Erase heading not required.*)

Army Form C. 2118.

Page 2.

Place	Date	Hour	Summary of Events and Information	Remarks and references to Appendices
STEENBECQUE	1/10/15	—	In Billets at STEENBECQUE (Reference $\frac{1}{100000}$ B 5.A.	
PRADELLES	2nd	—	do PRADELLES	
do	3rd	—	do do cleaning up, checking deficiences of kit	
"	4	—	do do do	
"	5	—	do do do & arranging Bde. hot baths	
"	6	—	do do do do	
"	7	—	do do do & instructing Inf. in trenching.	
"	8	—	do do do do	
"	9	—	do do do	
"	10	—	do do marched to COURTE RUE near NIEPPE	
COURTE RUE	11	—	In Camp at COURTE RUE. took up work on subsidiary line $\frac{1}{20000}$ 36 NW C_2-C_8	
"	12	—	do work as above, includes three closed works. CALVAIRE GRAND REBECQUE, & work in front.	
"	13	—	do	
"	14	—	do do	
"	15	—	do do	
"	16	—	do do detached No 3 Section to work at SEVEN TREES FORT	
"	17	—	do marched to ARMENTIERES & got billets – work as before	
ARMENTIERES	18	—	In Billets at ARMENTIERES, work as above	
"	19 to 31st Oct.		Same billets same work as above.	

J M Cloning RE

31/10/15 — OC 9 Fd Co RE

2353 Wt. W2544/1454 700,000 5/15 D. D. & L. A.D.S.S./Forms/C. 2118.

21st Division

98th F.C. R. E.
Vol: 3

121/7624

Nov 15

Instructions regarding War Diaries and Intelligence Summaries are contained in F. S. Regs., Part II. and the Staff Manual respectively. Title pages will be prepared in manuscript.

WAR DIARY
or
INTELLIGENCE SUMMARY.
(Erase heading not required.)

21st Dn

Army Form C. 2118.

3

Place	Date	Hour	Summary of Events and Information	Remarks and references to Appendices
ARMENTIERES	1st Nov		Work on subsidiary line GRAND RABECQUE and CALVAIRE continued	
do	2nd to 6th		— do — — do —	
do	7th		Took over trenches 67 to 73 inclusive from 2nd Northumbrian Field Co	
do	8th to 12th		Work on them; practically no decent dugouts existing, the parapet & communication trenches in very bad condition owing to lack of revetting during the summer months. Much labour appears to have been expended on useless "Shell trenches" which all fell in when the rain came. No 47156 Sapr Pelican C. wounded near HAYSTACK FARM on night of 12/11	
do	13th to 20th		Building dugouts, revetting all communication trenches, CENTRAL AVENUE abandoned as too bad for repair. No 97109 Sapr Way E.W. wounded while finishing dugout in trench 67 on 20/11	
do	20 to 30th		Gradual improvement showing in the sector — much still remains to be done & the supply of timber is absurdly inadequate.	

J M Clarke Major RE
OC 98 Fd Co RE

2353 Wt. W2544/1454 700,000 5/15 D. D. & L. A.D.S.S./Forms/C. 2118.

21st [illegible]

98th F.C.R.E.
Vol: 4

121
7910

Army Form C. 2118.

WAR DIARY
or
~~INTELLIGENCE SUMMARY~~.
(Erase heading not required.)

Instructions regarding War Diaries and Intelligence Summaries are contained in F. S. Regs., Part II. and the Staff Manual respectively. Title pages will be prepared in manuscript.

DECEMBER. 98th Field Company.

Place	Date	Hour	Summary of Events and Information	Remarks and references to Appendices
ARMENTIERES.				
	1st		Working on Trenches 67 to 73 inclusive, which are occupied by the 63 Inf. Bde. The 23rd Div on our right and 62nd Inf Bde. 21st Div on our left. Considerable difficulty experienced in draining the front and support lines and the communication Trenches. All drains have to be dug six feet deep and made very wide to avoid the sides falling in. The parapets and parados are apt to bulge and collapse, which entails a great deal of heavy labour.	
	[redacted]		Sergt BADRICK C. No 50140 killed.	
	4th.		98351 Sapr HALL G. wounded.	
	7th.		63576 2nd Cpl KNORR wounded.	
	8th.		51074 Sapr ANTHONY M. wounded.	
	15th.		8th SOMERSET L. I. carried out attack on the German Trenches from the MUSHROOM (Trench 70) We supplied various special stores for the attacking party notably a mat for crossing the wire entanglement. The mat was made of canvas 3' wide with gabion pickets nailed to one side of it and spaced 1½" apart. The length of the mat was 12 feet	

2353 Wt. W2544/1454 700,000 5/15 D. D. & L. A.D.S.S./Forms/C. 2118.

Instructions regarding War Diaries and Intelligence Summaries are contained in F. S. Regs., Part II. and the Staff Manual respectively. Title pages will be prepared in manuscript.

2

WAR DIARY
or
~~INTELLIGENCE SUMMARY~~.
(Erase heading not required.)

DECEMBER (contd). 98 Field Company

Army Form C. 2118.

Place	Date	Hour	Summary of Events and Information	Remarks and references to Appendices
	15 (Contd)		and was carried rolled up by one man. Six such mats were supplied & were found most useful. No men of the Company took part in the attack.	
			Lieut G. A. GREGSON wounded.	
	18th.		Major F. M. CLOSE promoted Temp Lt Colonel and Transferred to 14th Div as CRE. Captain R. E. DEWING assumed command of the Company.	
	19th.		The enemy exploded two mines 30x in front of the MUSHROOM (Trench 70). Much work carried out from now till the end of the month on Trenches and communications to command these CRATERS. All the work had to be done at night and was difficult on account of the wet state of the ground especially near the craters where the spoil from the explosions tended to slide into the craters. It is difficult to get ~~any~~ much useful help from the infantry. Sergts KELLYN and BAMBER and Lce Cpl TRUMPER did especially good work on this job.	
	31st.		The enemy did considerable damage to Trench 67 by shell fire.	
			Lieut N. AYRIS was killed while reconnoitring with a view to placing wire entanglement between the craters formed on the 19th.	
			Timber is scarce partly owing to the stoppage of the R. E. YARD sawmill	

8353 Wt. W2544/1454 700,000 5/15 D. D. & L. A.D.S.S./Forms/C. 2118.

Army Form C. 2118.

Instructions regarding War Diaries and Intelligence Summaries are contained in F. S. Regs., Part II. and the Staff Manual respectively. Title pages will be prepared in manuscript.

3

WAR DIARY
or
~~INTELLIGENCE SUMMARY.~~
(*Erase heading not required.*)

DECEMBER (contd)

98 Field Company.

Place	Date	Hour	Summary of Events and Information	Remarks and references to Appendices
			by floods. Corrugated iron also is extremely scarce. It is needed in large quantities for revetting, being the most suitable material for holding up the earth in its present slippery state. Drainage of the trenches has improved as a result of several drains being enlarged but there is still much water in some parts of the line. Work has been begun on the new scheme of defence by Company posts and a short portion of the line has been prepared for gas cylinders.	
			R E Drewry Capt RE OC 98 Fd RE	

8353 Wt. W2544/1454 700,000 5/15 D. D. & L. A.D.S.S./Forms/C. 2118.

21st Divisional Engine ers

98th FIELD COMPANY R. E. ::: JANUARY 1916.

98th F.C. R.B.
Vol: 5
Jan '16

21st D

Confidential

War Diary
of
98th Field Co. R. E
from Jan 1st – Jan 31st 1916

Volume 5

Instructions regarding War Diaries and Intelligence Summaries are contained in F. S. Regs., Part II. and the Staff Manual respectively. Title pages will be prepared in manuscript.

Army Form C. 2118.

WAR DIARY
or
INTELLIGENCE SUMMARY.
(*Erase heading not required.*)

1

JANUARY. 1916. 98 Field Company.

Place	Date	Hour	Summary of Events and Information	Remarks and references to Appendices
ARMENTIERES.				
	1st.		Still occupying the same part of the line. No work on Trench today. The company overhauled four barrel bridges for which we are responsible. A lot of work is required to make them serviceable.	
	2nd.		Lieut Gregson reported for duty.	
	3rd.		2/Lieut BULL joined from 8th Div. CHAPPELLE D'ARMENTIERES and LEITH WALK heavily shelled during afternoon.	
	6th.		Enemy shelled Trenches in morning. 2 sections worked on bridges near PONT NIEPPE instead of going to the Trenches.	
	17th		Capt Couchman took over command of the Co' from Capt Dewing	
	19th		Sapper Pillenger wounded on trench tramway	
	26th		2a Cpl TOCOCK wounded on trench tramway.	
	27		Sapper GAMMER wounded by shell in CHAPELLES D'ARMENTIERES.	
	31st		O.C. and 2/Lt Bull ~~went~~ to visit trenches 74 75 76 and part of 77 which are to be taken over on Feb 1st.	
			Squared timber is still short although much is wanted for the provision of revetting frames and gas cupboards. ~~Trenches~~ Fire and communication trenches are now all dry except in 2 or 3 places, a notable exception being	

$353 Wt. W2544/1454 700,000 5/15 D. D. & L. A.D.S.S./Forms/C. 2118.

Instructions regarding War Diaries and Intelligence Summaries are contained in F. S. Regs., Part II. and the Staff Manual respectively. Title pages will be prepared in manuscript.

Army Form C. 2118.

WAR DIARY
or
INTELLIGENCE SUMMARY.
(Erase heading not required.)

2/

Jan 1916 contd

Place	Date	Hour	Summary of Events and Information	Remarks and references to Appendices
ARMENTIERES			Trench 70 (known as the MUSHROOM) an advanced trench on low ground the draining of which presents great difficulty. Motor pumps are about to be installed at one or two points behind the line and it is hoped that we shall be able to cope with the next floods.	

[illegible] Capt.
[illegible]

2353 Wt. W2544/1454 700,000 5/15 D. D. & L. A.D.S.S./Forms/C. 2118.

21st Divisional Engineers

98th FIELD COMPANY R. E. ::: FEBRUARY 1916.

Confidential

War Diary

of

98 Field Company R. E.

from Feb 1st - 29th 1916

Volume VI

Instructions regarding War Diaries and Intelligence Summaries are contained in F. S. Regs., Part II. and the Staff Manual respectively. Title pages will be prepared in manuscript.

WAR DIARY

~~or~~

~~INTELLIGENCE SUMMARY.~~

(Erase heading not required.)

Army Form C. 2118.

98 Field Co RE — Feb 1916

Place	Date	Hour	Summary of Events and Information	Remarks and references to Appendices
ARMENTIERES	1st		From this date the Divisional front is being held by Two Brigades, with 3 Battalions each in front line only. This Field Co takes over Trenches 74, 75, 76 and part of 77 from 97 Field Co; this includes the EPINETTE salient (Trenches 75 & 76).	
			The Trenches are subdivided among the sections of the Field Co thus:-	
			No 1 Section Trenches 67 to 69 including LEITH WALK and LOTHIAN AV. No 4 Section Trenches 70 and 71 including CENTRAL AV. No 3 Section Trenches 72 to 74 including PORT EGAL AV. No 2 section 75, 76 and 77 (part) including PLANK AV and JAPAN ROAD.	
			Infantry Brigades ~~being~~ are relieved every 12 days (having 6 days in rest) and the Field Co ~~has therefore~~ no longer therefore works always with the same Brigade as before. This leads to a certain lack of continuity of policy.	
	6th to 29th		From this date Brigades have only Two Battalions in front line, this being split up into "company posts". The support line being now required to accommodate reserves, most of the Field Co. work for the rest of the month has been on this line which up to now has been an unrevetted trench, full of water. Through communication is first being	

2353 Wt. W2544/1454 700,000 5/15 D. D. & L. A.D.S.S./Forms/C. 2118.

Army Form C. 2118.

Instructions regarding War Diaries and Intelligence Summaries are contained in F. S. Regs., Part II. and the Staff Manual respectively. Title pages will be prepared in manuscript.

WAR DIARY

~~or~~

~~INTELLIGENCE~~ ~~SUMMARY.~~

(Erase heading not required.)

Place	Date	~~Hour~~ 20000	Map Sheet 36 NW — Summary of Events and Information	Remarks and references to Appendices
			made by laying trench boards, reclaiming & revetting following slowly behind.	
			During the month two 6" and two 4" motor pumps have been installed at following places I.16 b.0.4, I.10.b 6 7, I.10 c.6.8 and I.10 b.0.2 and in spite of a rise in the R. LYS during the month have coped with the water. They would do more good if the cross drains near front line were kept clear but no R.E can be spared for this and with Brigade reliefs it is difficult to impress the Infantry with the necessity for it. The MUSHROOM (Trench 70) though drier is still wet, and the stagnant water smells badly.	
	18th ~~Feb~~		2/Lieut F. HEWIN joined the Co from 46th Divn	
	24th	11 pm	10 York R attempted a cutting out enterprise but found enemy alert and had to retire. Lieut GREGSON R.E. with 2nd Corpl TRUMPER, Lance-Corporal STEWART, Sapper GEAR, and BALDWIN and Pioneer NORMAN, all of this Co, accompanied the party taking guncotton etc. Lieut GREGSON was wounded in the hand & leg and was evacuated the following morning	
	Feb 1st		Pioneer STEELE wounded	
	3rd		a/II CM NICKSON wounded	

2353 Wt. W2544/1454 700,000 5/15 D. D. & L. A.D.S.S./Forms/C. 2118.

Instructions regarding War Diaries and Intelligence Summaries are contained in F. S. Regs., Part II. and the Staff Manual respectively. Title pages will be prepared in manuscript.

WAR DIARY
or
~~INTELLIGENCE SUMMARY.~~

Feby 1916 cont^d (*Erase heading not required.*)

Army Form C. 2118.

Place	Date	Hour	Summary of Events and Information	Remarks and references to Appendices
	Feb 5		a/Cpl ROBINSON wounded	
	8th		Sapper STRIBBLING wounded	
	9th		Lce Cpl MASON. G. wounded	
	11th		Sapper CHAMBERS. W. killed. (with night working party)	
	22nd		Sergeant PITT. L. killed (" " " ")	
	24th		Lieut G. A. GREGSON wounded (q. v. ante)	
	27th		Lieut H. TAYLOR. killed by shell near HAYSTACK FARM	

[signature] Capt.
O.C. 98 F. Co R.E.

8353 Wt. W2544/1454 700,000 5/15 D. D. & L. A.D.S.S./Forms/C. 2118.

21st Divisional Engineers

98th FIELD COMPANY R. E. ::: MARCH 1916.

Confidential

War Diary

of

98th Field Company RE.

from March 1st – 31st 1916

Volume VII.

Instructions regarding War Diaries and Intelligence Summaries are contained in F. S. Regs., Part II. and the Staff Manual respectively. Title pages will be prepared in manuscript.

Army Form C. 2118.

WAR DIARY
or
INTELLIGENCE SUMMARY.

98 Field Co RE (*Erase heading not required.*) March 1916.

Place	Date	Hour	Summary of Events and Information	Remarks and references to Appendices
ARMENTIERES	1st		Still occupying same part of line. 34th Division is now on our right.	
	2nd		Lieut E.L.V. DAKIN joined the Co. Sapper CHESTERS killed when on night working party.	
	1st – 19th		Same work as during latter part of February except that we make a start at making good the MUSHROOM Trench 70, which had been allowed by the infantry to fall into disrepair. ~~The~~ The parapet is being revetted with wooden  frames, ~~and~~ raised & thickened as it is not bullet proof. A new short drain has been cut and other drains cleared & deepened.	
	18th – 20th		Weather warm ~~Weather~~ The 17th Division having relieved the 21st Division here, work on front trenches has been handed over to 77th Field Co R.E. Handing over was spread over 3 days with gradually increasing numbers of the relieving Co and gradually decreasing numbers of this Co at work each day.	
	20th		With C.E. II Corps to see site of wire entanglement round ARMENTIERES which the Co is to do. Weather cold again.	
	21st	9.30pm	Wiring started with 3 sections working from 9.30 p.m to 5.30 a.m. Work is about C.27.b. and C.22c. where it would be unwise to work by day. No 2 Section remain at work in Trenches 74 to 77 until relieved as 77 Field Co have only taken over trenches 67 to 73 (Right Brigade area)	

2353 Wt. W2544/1454 700,000 5/15 D. D. & L. A.D.S.S./Forms/C. 2118.

Army Form C. 2118.

WAR DIARY
or
INTELLIGENCE SUMMARY.
(Erase heading not required.)

Instructions regarding War Diaries and Intelligence Summaries are contained in F. S. Regs., Part II. and the Staff Manual respectively. Title pages will be prepared in manuscript.

98 Field Co — March 1916 (continued)

Place	Date	Hour	Sheet 36 (1/40000) Summary of Events and Information	Remarks and references to Appendices
ARMENTIERES	23rd		No 2 Section, relieved by part of 78th Field Co, begin wiring.	
	30th		Finished wiring. Packing wagons for move next day.	
	31st	9.30 a.m.	Marched. Billeted in BAILLEUL.	

[signature] Captain
OC 98 F Co

2353 Wt. W2544/1454 700,000 5/15 D. D. & L. A.D.S.S./Forms/C. 2118.

21st Divisional Engineers

98th FIELD COMPANY R. E. ::: APRIL 1916.

98 F C R E
Army Form C. 2118.
Vol 8

XXI

WAR DIARY
or
~~INTELLIGENCE SUMMARY.~~

Instructions regarding War Diaries and Intelligence Summaries are contained in F. S. Regs., Part II. and the Staff Manual respectively. Title pages will be prepared in manuscript.

98 Field Co RE (Erase heading not required.) April 1916

Place	Date	Hour	Summary of Events and Information	Remarks and references to Appendices
BAILLEUL	1st	8.15 a.m	Marched. Entrained at GODEWAERSVELDE 11.30 to 12.30 p.m. In train rest of day	
ALLONVILLE	2nd		Detrained at LONGUEAU (near AMIENS) at 2 a.m. Marched to ALLONVILLE. Into billets there. Weather very fine. This is fortunate as men can sleep out, billets being bad.	
"	3rd to 6th		Work in mornings, pontooning, map reading, drill & odd jobs. Weather colder from 4th	
"				
BUIRE sur L'ANCRE	7th		Left ALLONVILLE 9.30 a.m. Arrived BUIRE 2.0 p.m. Into billets	
"	8th to 21st		Work on improving billets & horse lines, erecting huts, also route marching. Weather fine then wet	
"	21st - 30th		Weather very fine. Work as before. Capt DEWING R.E. of the Co. supervising work of part of 126 Field Co RE in trenches for last fortnight of the month	

[signature] Capt RE
OC 98 F Co RE

30.4.16

8353 Wt. W2544/1454 700,000 5/15 D. D. & L. A.D.S.S./Forms/C. 2118.

21st Divisional Engineers

98th FIELD COMPANY R. E. ::: MAY 1916.

Confidential

War Diary

of

98th Field Co R.E

from

May 1st – 31st 1916

Vol IX

98 F. C. R.E.

Army Form C. 2118.

Vol. 9

Vol IX

WAR DIARY

or

~~INTELLIGENCE SUMMARY.~~

98th Field Co RE (Erase heading not required.) May 1916.

XXI

Instructions regarding War Diaries and Intelligence Summaries are contained in F. S. Regs., Part II. and the Staff Manual respectively. Title pages will be prepared in manuscript.

Place	Date	Hour	Summary of Events and Information	Remarks and references to Appendices
BUIRE	1st – 13th		Work in and around BUIRE erecting huts, building trestle bridges (two) over River ANCRE and odd jobs generally	
	14th to 31st		Two sections (1 & 4) move to the trenches on 14th to live & work there. One of them employed principally on making deep dugouts, the other on pipe-line, and improving new communication trenches.	
			Remaining two sections at BUIRE, one section on deep dugouts, ~~[illegible]~~ the other on odd jobs which tend to increase. Weather generally very fine.	
	28th		Capt DEWING left on transfer as O C 223rd Field Co.	
			No casualties during month	

[signature] Capt RE

O.C. 98 F. Co. RE

1. 6. 16.

2353 Wt. W2544/1454 700,000 5/15 D. D. & L. A.D.S.S./Forms/C. 2118.

21st Divisional Engineers

98th FIELD COMPANY R. E. ::: JUNE 1916

Confidential

War Diary

of

98th Field Co. R.E.

from

June 1st – 30th 1916

Volume X

DAG.

3rd Echelon.

Herewith Vol X of War Diary of this Co.

[illegible signature]
Captain

30.6.16.

O.C. 98 F Co RE

98 F.C. RE

Army Form C. 2118.

XXI

Vol 10

Instructions regarding War Diaries and Intelligence Summaries are contained in F. S. Regs., Part II. and the Staff Manual respectively. Title pages will be prepared in manuscript.

WAR DIARY
~~or~~
~~INTELLIGENCE SUMMARY.~~

98th Field Co RE (Erase heading not required.)

June 1916.

Place	Date	Hour	Summary of Events and Information	Remarks and references to Appendices
BUIRE-SUR-ANCRE	4th		Lieut W.L. CAMPBELL joined the Co.	
	1st – 24th		Nos 1 & 4 Section working in the trenches as last month. No 3 Section principally employed on deep dugouts for advanced Div H.Q. No 2 Section on various works in & about BUIRE.	
	24th		Bombardment of enemy trenches began. No 1 Section moved back to BUIRE in evening. No 4 remains to carry out repairs to pipe line & trenches	
	27th	8.15pm	Nos 2 & 3 Section move up to dugouts in Queens Redoubt	
	30th		O.C moved to dugout in Queen's Redoubt leaving headquarters and No 1 Sec in BUIRE.	

[signature] Capt R.E.

O.C. 98 F. Co RE

30.6.16

21st Divisional Engineers

98th FIELD COMPANY R. E. ::: JULY 1916.

98 FCRE
Vol 11

Confidential

War Diary

of

98th Field Co R.E.

21st Division

from July 1st – 31st 1916

Volume XI.

Army Form C. 2118.

WAR DIARY
~~or~~
~~INTELLIGENCE SUMMARY.~~

Instructions regarding War Diaries and Intelligence Summaries are contained in F. S. Regs., Part II. and the Staff Manual respectively. Title pages will be prepared in manuscript.

98th Field Co R. E. (Erase heading not required.) July 1916

Place	Date	Hour	Summary of Events and Information	Remarks and references to Appendices
			Sheet 1/20000 MONTAUBAN	
BECOURT VALLEY	1st	7 30 a.m	Nos 2 & 3 Sections with D Co 14 N.F (Pioneers) & 100 men 13th Northd Fus (carrying party) to front line trench. One casualty before moving off. Remained there until 10.30 p.m. ordered to make 4 strong points along line FRICOURT FARM - LOZENGE ALLEY, one Section 126 Fd Co RE and 2 platoons B. Co 14 N F (P) being attached for this. Guided one party to its objective. Remaining parties failed to find theirs as shell fire prevented movement above ground & trenches were blocked by movement of troops. Returned at daybreak. 5 casualties from shell fire. Nos 1 & 4 Section under Major PHILL-POTTS RE dug communication trench across NO MANS LAND	
"	2nd	9.45 p.m	The Company with D. Co & 1 platoon C Co 14 N.F (Pioneers) moved out to deepen & improve communication trench from DINET ST (X.26.b.4.6) along PATCH ALLEY to SUNKEN Road (X. 27.b). Returned to BECOURT VALLEY at 5.30 a.m. No casualties.	
	3rd	5.45 p.m	Company with 1½ Co [Pioneers] moved off to CRUCIFIX Trench (X. 27.b.). Worked on two small strong points at X.27.b.8.4 and X.28.c.2.7 Deepened & wired CRUCIFIX trench between these points and deepened new trench from ~~latter~~ former point to SUNKEN Road. No casualties. Returned at 3.30 a.m.	
Map 1/100000 Sheet 17 (AMIENS)	4th		Relieved by 17th Division. Left BECOURT VALLEY 7.30 a.m. arrived DERNANCOURT siding 9.15 a.m & remained there until 8. p.m. Heavy rain & no shelter. Entrained. Transport under Lt DAKIN RE. by road from BUIRE to FREMONT	
FREMONT	5th		Detrained AILLY-SUR-SOMME 1 a.m, remained in station until 7.0 a.m. arrived FREMONT 8.30 a.m. Into billets.	

3353 Wt. W2544/1454 700,000 5/15 D. D. & L. A.D.S.S./Forms/C. 2118.

Army Form C. 2118.

WAR DIARY

or

~~INTELLIGENCE SUMMARY.~~

(Erase heading not required.)

Instructions regarding War Diaries and Intelligence Summaries are contained in F. S. Regs., Part II. and the Staff Manual respectively. Title pages will be prepared in manuscript.

Map 1/100000 Sheet 17 (AMIENS)

Place	Date	Hour	Summary of Events and Information — 98 Field Co RE — July 1916	Remarks and references to Appendices
FREMONT	6th		In billets. fine	
	7th	3.0pm	Marched via PICQUIGNY and SOUES to Farm halfway between SOUES and HANGEST	
HANGEST	8th		In billets. Inspected by G.O.C 21 Div.	
	9th	2.0pm	Transport under Lieut DAKIN marched to QUERRIEU.	
	10th	4.0pm	Dismounted men marched to AILLY-SUR-SOMME. Entrained 9.30 p.m. Detrained CORBIE. By bus to VILLE. Transport marched to VILLE.	
VILLE-SOUS-CORBIE	11th		Camped	
	12th		Dismounted men marched to BECOURT VALLEY in morning. Moved out at 6 pm to MAMETZ WOOD and made 4 strong points along north and east edges. (1 Co Pioneers attached)	
BECOURT VALLEY	13th		Returned from work 8 a.m. No 2 Section moved out 8.30 p m to erect screen between MAMETZ and BAZENTIN-LE-PETIT Woods. (1 Platoon Pioneers attached)	
	14th		~~Moved out at 2.0 a.m~~ No 1, 3 & 4 Secns moved out at 2.0 a.m (with D. Co 14 N.F. Pioneers) Halted south of MAMETZ WOOD until 8.0 a.m. Moved to main German line between MAMETZ and BAZENTIN-LE-PETIT Woods and made 3 strong points there; also deepened communication trench between this line & MAMETZ Wood. Casualties 3 killed 19 wounded 1 missing. Returned to BECOURT Valley 9.0 p.m. During day transport moved from VILLE to field just east of FRICOURT.	

8353 Wt. W2544/1454 700,000 5/15 D. D. & L. A.D.S.S./Forms/C. 2118.

Army Form C. 2118.

Instructions regarding War Diaries and Intelligence Summaries are contained in F. S. Regs., Part II. and the Staff Manual respectively. Title pages will be prepared in manuscript.

WAR DIARY

~~or~~

~~INTELLIGENCE SUMMARY.~~

(Erase heading not required.)

Place	Date	Hour	Summary of Events and Information — 98 Field Co RE — July 1916	Remarks and references to Appendices
near FRICOURT	15th		Section joined transport about noon. In bivouac.	
"	16th		Section with 2 Cos Pioneers moved out at 4.0 a.m to BAZENTIN-LE-PETIT Wood and completed 4 strong points there, made new one in the village and wired round east edge of wood. Returned 5.30 pm. One casualty	
"	17th		In bivouac	
Ville-sous-Corbie	18th	1.30 pm	Marched to VILLE-sous-CORBIE & bivouacked.	
	19th	4.30pm	Marched to ALLONVILLE arrived 10 p.m.	
ALLONVILLE	20th		In billets	
"	21st		" "	
	22nd	8.30 a.m	Marched to LONGUEAU. Entrained 12 noon. ~~Arr~~ Detrained ST. POL 7 p.m. Marched to MONTS-EN-TERNOIS arrived 9.30 p.m. (Whole Co & transport left station yard within one hour of arrival.)	
MONTS-EN-TERNOIS	23rd		In billets	
"	24th		Marched 6.15 p.m. Arrived BLAVINCOURT 9 p.m into billets	
BLAVINCOURT	25th		In billets	
	26th		In billets. O.C. to ARRAS & back to see new sector of line.	
	27th		In billets	

#353 Wt. W2544/1454 700,000 5/15 D. D. & L. A.D.S.S./Forms/C. 2118.

Army Form C. 2118.

WAR DIARY
~~or~~
~~INTELLIGENCE SUMMARY.~~

Instructions regarding War Diaries and Intelligence Summaries are contained in F. S. Regs., Part II. and the Staff Manual respectively. Title pages will be prepared in manuscript.

98 Field Co R.E. (Erase heading not required.) July 1916.

Place	Date	Hour	Summary of Events and Information	Remarks and references to Appendices
BLAVINCOURT	28th		Left in lorries 7 p.m arrived ARRAS 10.30 p.m. Into billets. Transport marched to MONTENESCOURT	
ARRAS	29th		In billets. Took over 'K' sector of Trenches from 89th Field Co, 14th Division. R.E work at present is principally on deep dugouts. These are mainly 100 to 200 yards behind the front line. Section Officers reconnoitring the Trenches	
"	30th		NCO's taken round the Trenches	
"	31st		Work started Weather very hot	

[signature] Capt R.E.
O.C. 98 Fd Co RE

31. 7. 16

$353 Wt. W2544/1454 700,000 5/15 D. D. & L. A.D.S.S./Forms/C. 2118.

21st Divisional Engineers

98th FIELD COMPANY R. E. ::: AUGUST 1916.

Vol 12

Secret

War Diary

of

98th Field Co R.E

from

Aug 1st – 31st 1916

Volume XII

Instructions regarding War Diaries and Intelligence Summaries are contained in F. S. Regs., Part II. and the Staff Manual respectively. Title pages will be prepared in manuscript.

WAR DIARY ~~or~~ ~~INTELLIGENCE SUMMARY.~~

Army Form C. 2118.

98th Field Co RE (Erase heading not required.) August 1916.

Place	Date	Hour	Summary of Events and Information	Remarks and references to Appendices
ARRAS	1st – 31st		Work continued throughout month on trenches in K Sector of Divisional front (Trenches 102 to 125 both inclusive). 64 Inf Bde hold this portion of the line. In addition to four deep dugouts (one of which was completed during month) work has mainly been on the two main communication trenches, which are being graded, deepened where necessary & trenchboards laid. Some portions have been revetted with timber U frames 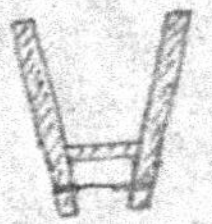 with corrugated iron behind. Much remains to be done.	
			A disused trench (Trench 40) running from SUNDAY Avenue to LILLE Road has been taken in hand, traverses & firebays practically completed over ~~half~~ nearly half the length. 200 men of VI Corps Cyclist Bn employed on this under R.E. supervision.	
			100 Infantry from Bns of 64 Inf Bde were attached to this Co for a month from Aug 16th as working party. This arrangement has proved a success as the men naturally take more interest in their work.	
			On Aug 26th orders received to make emplacements for gas cylinders along K 2 (left) sector of Bde sector. Previous experience having shown the impracticability of making up boxes & carrying them into front trenches, we made	

Army Form C. 2118.

Instructions regarding War Diaries and Intelligence Summaries are contained in F. S. Regs., Part II. and the Staff Manual respectively. Title pages will be prepared in manuscript.

WAR DIARY

~~or~~

~~INTELLIGENCE SUMMARY.~~

(*Erase heading not required.*)

Place	Date	Hour	Summary of Events and Information	Remarks and references to Appendices
			end frames only 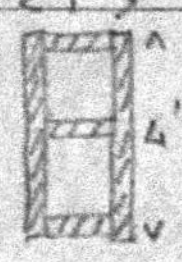 of 3" x 2" ~~[illegible]~~ spur in corrugated iron behind + in front ~~[illegible]~~ with 1½" plank on top + bottom. In one or two cases the parapets fell in + had to be rebuilt but once the frames are in + loose stuff packed in behind the corrugated iron there seems little danger of a collapse. We were ordered to complete by night of Sept 1st – 2nd but as an extra emplacement was asked for at last moment we did not complete until 4 p.m. Sept 2nd. No casualties during month. [illegible] Capt RE O.C. 98th Fd. Co. RE.	

8353 Wt. W2544/1454 700,000 5/15 D. D. & L. A.D.S.S./Forms/C. 2118.

21st Divisional Engineers

98th FIELD COMPANY R. E. ::: SEPTEMBERV 1916.

21 Div

Confidential

War Diary
of
98th Field Co R.E.

Sept 1st – 30th 1916

Volume XIII

Instructions regarding War Diaries and Intelligence Summaries are contained in F. S. Regs., Part II. and the Staff Manual respectively. Title pages will be prepared in manuscript.

Army Form C. 2118.

Vol 13

WAR DIARY
or
~~INTELLIGENCE SUMMARY~~.

98th Field Co R.E. (Erase heading not required.) September 1916

Place	Date	Hour	Summary of Events and Information	Remarks and references to Appendices
ARRAS	Sept 2nd		Went round K sector of trenches with O.C. 205 Fd Co. The Co relieves us	
"	3rd		Subalterns of 205 Fd Co round the trenches to see work going on.	
	4th		Dismounted men left ARRAS in small parties during afternoon and marched to NOYELLETTE. O.C. left 9 p.m.	
NOYELLETTE	5th	1.30 pm	Marched to BLAVINCOURT. Into billets.	
BLAVIN-COURT	6th – 11th		In billets, weather fine. Co doing route marches, pontooning and other training.	
"	12th	10.30 am	Marched to FAMECHON with Transport of 110th Inf Bde. O.C. in command of column.	
FAME-CHON	13th	9 am	Marched to bivouac about 1 mile N W of DERNANCOURT. Long march.	
DERNAN-COURT	14th		In bivouac	
	15th	7.45 am	Marched to new bivouac in DERNANCOURT.	
	"	5 pm	Marched to new bivouac FRICOURT Camp.	

2353 Wt. W2544/1454 700,000 5/15 D. D. & L. A.D.S.S./Forms/C. 2118.

Instructions regarding War Diaries and Intelligence Summaries are contained in F. S. Regs., Part II. and the Staff Manual respectively. Title pages will be prepared in manuscript.

Army Form C. 2118.

WAR DIARY
or
~~INTELLIGENCE SUMMARY.~~
(Erase heading not required.)

98th Field Co   Sept 1916

Place	Date	Hour	Summary of Events and Information	Remarks and references to Appendices
FRICOURT CAMP	16th	10pm	~~Halted ...~~ Marched to new bivouac about 1 mile north of CARNOY in old NO MANS LAND.	
1 mile N. of CARNOY	17th -20th		In bivouac, weather generally wet. Co working each night on a new communication trench (GUN ALLEY) through squares T.1.b & N.32.c. Men go to LONGUEVAL in pontoon & limber wagons & return. Had about 12 casualties on night 17th-18th including 2 missing believed killed. On night 20th-21st carried up RE stores to advanced dump in preparation for offensive.	
	21st	5.15 pm.	Marched to new bivouac in valley close to BERNAFAY WOOD. Carried up RE stores.	
BERNAFAY WOOD	22nd -23rd		In bivouac. Work continued on GUN ALLEY	
	24th, 25		Rest. 21st Division attacked GIRD Trench & GUEUDECOURT. Co. had been ordered to make strong points in the village but couldn't be sent there as village was not taken. Moved out at 9 p.m to dig fire trench connecting our left in GIRD Trench with centre in old front line. 1 Co of Pioneer Bn attached. Greater part of the Co lost touch & did not reach objective. Dug 250 yards of trench. 2nd Lieut J W BULL severely wounded and 6 O.R.	

2353 Wt. W2544/1454 700,000 5/15 D. D. & L. A.D.S.S./Forms/C. 2118.

Instructions regarding War Diaries and Intelligence Summaries are contained in F. S. Regs., Part II. and the Staff Manual respectively. Title pages will be prepared in manuscript.

WAR DIARY

or

~~INTELLIGENCE SUMMARY.~~

(Erase heading not required.)

Army Form C. 2118.

98 Field Co — Septr 1916.

Place	Date	Hour	Summary of Events and Information	Remarks and references to Appendices
BERNAFAY WOOD.	26th	"	Moved out 6 30 pm to GUEUDECOURT to make 4 strong points. 1 Co of Pioneer Bn and 2 sec^ns 97 Fd Co attached. The 2 sec^ns 97 Fd Co and 3 platoons Pioneers detailed for 2 points were shelled and unable to do much work. Sec^n of this Co with 1 platoon Pioneers completed 2 strong points without enemy interference.	
	27th		Completed remaining 2 strong points in GUEUDECOURT. Except for a heavy burst of shelling lasting ½ hour the night was fairly quiet. 3 platoons Pioneers attached.	
	28th – 30th		Continued work on GUN ALLEY.	
			During the offensive, casualties in N C O's have been out of all proportion to total number. 1 Sergeant 2 Corporals 2 2nd Corporals & 2 Lance Corporals have been wounded & evacuated and 3 Lance Corporals slightly wounded. 1 Sergeant has been evacuated sick.	

[illegible] Captain
OC 98 F Co RE.

2353 Wt. W2544/1454 700,000 5/15 D. D. & L. A.D.S.S./Forms/C. 2118.

21st Divisional Engineers

98th FIELD COMPANY R. E. ::: OCTOBER 1916.

Army Form C. 2118.

Vol 14

WAR DIARY
~~or~~
~~INTELLIGENCE SUMMARY.~~

Instructions regarding War Diaries and Intelligence Summaries are contained in F. S. Regs., Part II. and the Staff Manual respectively. Title pages will be prepared in manuscript.

98th Field Co RE (Erase heading not required.) Oct 1916.

Place	Date	Hour	Summary of Events and Information	Remarks and references to Appendices
BERNAFAY Wood	Oct 1st		Rest. Orders as to relief of 21st Divn received.	
"	2nd	8.0 a.m.	Marched to DERNANCOURT and bivouached there. Weather wet.	
DERNANCOURT	3rd		In bivouac. Transport + cyclists marched to ARGOEVES. Weather wet	
"	4th	8.0 pm	~~Ent~~ Dismounted portion of Co: entrained at DERNANCOURT after waiting 4 hours at station. Transport etc marched to PONT REMY. Weather wet	
PONT REMY	5th		Detrained at LONGPRE 3.30 a.m and marched to billets, 7 miles Weather fine	
"	6th 7th		In billets. Weather changeable.	
"	8th	12.0 noon	Entrained with all transport. Detrained at BETHUNE 8.0 p.m and marched to VERQUIGNEUL 3 miles.	
VERQUIGNEUL	9th		In billets. O.C + 4 officers to NOYELLES to go round trenches with officers of 1st Home Counties Field Co 8th Divn from whom we take over.	
"	10th	2.30 pm	Marched to NOYELLES. Into billets.	
NOYELLES	11th		Officers + NCOs of Co to visit the trenches + work in hand. This is almost entirely deep dugouts ~~and~~ & a few other odd jobs being in hand.	

8353 Wt. W2544/1454 700,000 5/15 D. D. & L. A.D.S.S./Forms/C. 2118.

Instructions regarding War Diaries and Intelligence Summaries are contained in F. S. Regs., Part II. and the Staff Manual respectively. Title pages will be prepared in manuscript.

WAR DIARY

~~or~~

~~INTELLIGENCE SUMMARY.~~

(Erase heading not required.)

Army Form C. 2118.

98th Field Co — October 1916.

Place	Date	Hour	Summary of Events and Information	Remarks and references to Appendices
NOYELLES	11th contd		The Co works in the 110th Bde Sector which is the HOHENZOLLERN and includes the numerous craters. Front & support line trenches are very bad in places, & nowhere good. Communication trenches fair but unrevetted.	
"	12th		Some work started but NCO's & men mainly employed in visiting trenches & learning their way about. Stores sent up at night. No. 3 Section working under CRE on hutting etc in back area.	
"	13th		Work in full swing	
	17th		110th Bde take over about 400 yards of line from 64th Bde on left and hand over same amount to 62nd Bde on left. Work stopped on 3 dugouts in latter area.	
	18th to ~~24~~ 26th		Work continued. Supply of material is good & timber at present plentiful. Weather very cold then wet and as a result of this trenches are beginning to fall in badly, aided by enemy trench mortar activity.	
	27th		Capt COUCHMAN ~~goes~~ leaves the company to take the place of the CRE away on other duties. Lt SCHWAB takes over command of company. Weather wet and Trenches in a very bad condition.	
	28th to 31st		Work on dugouts continued and work on trench shelters commenced. Weather wet with a few fine intervals	

M H Schwab
OC. 98th Fd Coy RE.

8353 Wt. W2544/1454 700,000 5/15 D. D. & L. A.D.S.S./Forms/C. 2118.

21st Divisional Engineers

98th FIELD COMPANY R. E. :: NOVEMBER 1916.

"CONFIDENTIAL"

WAR DIARY

of

98th FIELD COMPANY, R.E.

Vol 15

FROM 1st Nov 1916 To 30th Nov 1916.

Instructions regarding War Diaries and Intelligence Summaries are contained in F. S. Regs., Part II. and the Staff Manual respectively. Title pages will be prepared in manuscript.

WAR DIARY
or
~~INTELLIGENCE SUMMARY.~~

98th Field Coy. R.E. (*Erase heading not required.*) November 1916

Army Form C. 2118.

Place	Date	Hour	Summary of Events and Information	Remarks and references to Appendices
NOYELLES-LES-VERMELLES	Nov 8th		Captain COUCHMAN returned to the Co.	
	Nov 1st - 30th		Work in HOHENZOLLERN Sector continued throughout the month, principally on the dugouts started by 8th Div. The majority of these are nearing completion and some have been finished. One dugout was blown in by minenwerfer bombs early in the month, the two entrances, which had been (wrongly) made in the same bay, being blocked by one bomb, the emergency exit in rear by another and the roof of the chamber broken by a third. The two men in the dugout at the time crawled out through the hole in the roof unhurt. Several splinterproof shelters are being made in the Reserve Line where there is ~~both~~ no accommodation at present. Supply of material remains good. Corrugated iron, of which considerable quantities are being used for revetment, was scarce for a few days but is now plentiful. From Nov 28th 3 shifts are being worked on the dugouts in the front and close support line where accommodation is badly needed but Sappers and Infantry are not available for more than 2 shifts on dugouts in Reserve Line.	
			The weather has on the whole been good throughout the month, but very much	

Instructions regarding War Diaries and Intelligence Summaries are contained in F. S. Regs., Part II. and the Staff Manual respectively. Title pages will be prepared in manuscript.

WAR DIARY
or
INTELLIGENCE SUMMARY.
(Erase heading not required.)

Army Form C. 2118.

Place	Date	Hour	Summary of Events and Information	Remarks and references to Appendices
			has resulted in much falling in of trenches.	
NOYELLES	Nov 25		Captain COUCHMAN promoted to rank of Major.	
"	27		Lieut A WILLIAMSON joined the Co, being attached from the 197th Co RE.	

[illegible] Major RE.
OC 98 Field Co RE.

8353 Wt. W2544/1454 700,000 5/15 D. D. & L. A.D.S.S./Forms/C. 2118.

21st Divisional Engineers

98th FIELD COMPANY R. E. :::: DECEMBER 1916.

Vol 16

CONFIDENTIAL

WAR DIARY

OF

98TH FIELD COY RE

FROM 1ST DECR. 1916 TO 30TH DECR 1916

Army Form C. 2118.

WAR DIARY
or
~~INTELLIGENCE~~ SUMMARY.

Instructions regarding War Diaries and Intelligence Summaries are contained in F. S. Regs., Part II. and the Staff Manual respectively. Title pages will be prepared in manuscript.

98th Field Co RE (Erase heading not required.) Dec 1916

Place	Date	Hour	Summary of Events and Information	Remarks and references to Appendices
NOYELLES	1st -17th		Work continued in HOHENZOLLERN Sector. Weather has generally been fair.	
	8th		Lieut. M.H. SCHWAB left the Co. on transfer to 104th Field Co as 2nd in command.	
	14th		2nd Lieut G. HEPBURN joined the Co.	
	15th		64th Inf Bde relieved 110th Inf Bde in HOHENZOLLERN Sector.	
	17th		Major W.H.S. COUCHMAN acts as C.R.E. during absence of Lt. Col. C. Coffin R.E. Capt E.L.V. DAKIN commands the Co.	
	23rd		Officers of 1st London RE(T) Coy were shown round Sector and shown work in progress.	
	26th		Handed over to the 1st London RE(T) Coy and the Coy moved to RAIMBERT via NOEUX-LES-MINES BRUAY and AUCHEL and were billeted in miners dwellings.	
	27th		Work on Horse lines and general cleaning.	
	28th -30th		Training in Squad drill + rifle exercises.	

E.L.V. Dakin Capt RE
OC 98th Coy RE

2353 Wt. W2544/1454 700,000 5/15 D. D. & L. A.D.S.S./Forms/C. 2118.

CONFIDENTIAL

Vol 17

WAR DIARY

OF

98TH FIELD COMPANY RE

FROM. JANRY 2ND 1917. TO JANRY 31st 1917.

98th Field Co. R.E.

Army Form C. 2118.

WAR DIARY
or
~~INTELLIGENCE SUMMARY.~~

Instructions regarding War Diaries and Intelligence Summaries are contained in F. S. Regs., Part II. and the Staff Manual respectively. Title pages will be prepared in manuscript.

98th Field Co RE (Erase heading not required.)

Jany 1917.

Place	Date	Hour	Summary of Events and Information	Remarks and references to Appendices
RAIMBERT	Jan 2nd		No. 3 Section under Lt HEPBURN to MAZINGARBE in busses in morning, One section of all 3 Field Cos having been detailed to work in trenches under C.R.E. Capt DAKIN of this Co also goes in general charge of work.	
	3rd		Co. route march	
	4th		Major COUCHMAN returned to the Co. Very wet	
	5th		Drill in morning. All available men marched to AUCHEL in afternoon to hear R.E. Band	
	6th		Cleaning wagons & checking equipment.	
	7th		Sunday. No work.	
	8th		Co. route march. Snow & rain especially in afternoon.	
	9th		Major COUCHMAN acts as CRE. Lt CAMPBELL relieved Capt DAKIN in MAZINGARBE.	
	10th – 17th		Company employed on drill, route marches, erection of service trestle etc.	
	18th		Major COUCHMAN returned to the Co. Lt Col ADDISON, CRE visited Co. Very cold	
	20th		Major COUCHMAN to ~~[illegible]~~ course of Field Co Commanders near G.H.Q. No. 3 Section with Lieut CAMPBELL & Lt HEPBURN returned to the Co on completion of work.	
	21st		Sunday. No work.	
	22nd		Capt. DAKIN rejoined company.	
	23rd		Capt DAKIN to LES BREBIS to arrange for taking over from 104th Fd Coy.	
	24th		Co. route march. Hard frost.	
	25th		Co. sports.	

2353 Wt. W2544/1454 700,000 5/15 D. D. & L. A.D.S.S./Forms/C. 2118.

Army Form C. 2118.

WAR DIARY
~~or~~
~~INTELLIGENCE SUMMARY.~~

Instructions regarding War Diaries and Intelligence Summaries are contained in F. S. Regs., Part II. and the Staff Manual respectively. Title pages will be prepared in manuscript.

98th Field Co, R.E. (Erase heading not required.) Jan. 1917

Place	Date	Hour	Summary of Events and Information	Remarks and references to Appendices
RAIMBERT	26th		Co. employed on packing up & cleaning billets. II Lts HEPBURN & McLAREN with advance party to LOOS to take over from 104th Fd Coy	
		9pm	Orders received to stop all movement with regard to relief.	
	27th	8.30am	Orders received for transport to proceed to NEUF BERQUIN	
		10am	Transport left. Lt WILLIAMSON left to become second in command of 12th Fd. Coy, R.E.	
		1pm	Orders received for remainder of coy. to entrain at LILLERS at 19.07	
		5pm	Coy. marched to LILLERS & entrained	
	28th	2am	Coy detrained at PROVEN & marched to billets in farms at WINNEZEELE.	
WINNEZEELE J.11a 6.9 (Sheet 27).			Transport arrived 4pm, with II Lts HEPBURN & McLAREN.	
	29th		Coy. rested. Hard frost	
	30th		Drill & work about billets. Slight snow.	
	31st		Drill & musketry training.	

E W Walker Capt RE
O/C 98th Fd Coy RE
2/17

8353 Wt. W2544/1454 700,000 5/15 D. D. & L. A.D.S.S./Forms/C. 2118.

Vol 18

Confidential

War Diary

of

98th Field Co RE

21st Division

from Feb 1st - 28th 1917

Vol XVIII

Army Form C. 2118.

WAR DIARY

or

~~INTELLIGENCE SUMMARY.~~

Instructions regarding War Diaries and Intelligence Summaries are contained in F. S. Regs., Part II. and the Staff Manual respectively. Title pages will be prepared in manuscript.

98th Field Co R.E. (Erase heading not required.) February 1917.

Place	Date	Hour	Summary of Events and Information	Remarks and references to Appendices
WINNE-ZEELE	Jan 31st		Major COUCHMAN returned to the Co from Course of instruction.	
"	Feb 1st		Drill etc.	
"	2nd		Drill etc. Officers & NCOs ~~lay out~~ select sites for & lay out a strong point	
"	3rd		Drill morning. Route march to WATOU in afternoon by Brigade orders	
"	4th		Sunday. Officers & NCOs to select sites for strong points in scheme set by CRE. Route march as on 3rd	
"	5th		Drill morning. Route march as on 3rd	
"	6th		Test turn out ordered by Division. Co with all wagons turned out ready to march off in 1 hr 28 mins.	
"	7th		Drill etc.	
"	8th		Dismounted ~~[illegible]~~ men to sites of strong points selected. C.R.E. visited sites & explained scheme.	
"	9th		CRE visited Co. in morning and gave lecture on R.E. work in 1914.	
"	10th		Drill etc. The weather has been very cold with frost all the month. First sign of thaw today.	
"	11th		Sunday no work.	
"	12th		Transport moved at noon to HAZEBROUCK. Dismounted men with cooks cart remain.	

8353 Wt. W2544/1454 700,000 5/15 D. D. & L. A.D.S.S./Forms/C. 2118.

Instructions regarding War Diaries and Intelligence Summaries are contained in F. S. Regs., Part II. and the Staff Manual respectively. Title pages will be prepared in manuscript.

Army Form C. 2118.

WAR DIARY
or
~~INTELLIGENCE SUMMARY.~~
(Erase heading not required.)

98th Field Co RE — Feb 1917 (cont'd)

Place	Date	Hour	Summary of Events and Information	Remarks and references to Appendices
WINNEZEELE	Feb 13th		Dismounted men marched to PROVEN 3.45 a.m. On arrival loaded infantry wagons on to trucks & entrained. Detrained & unloaded wagons at CHOCQUES at 2 p.m. marched to BETHUNE & billeted. Weather mild. Transport marched to BELLE RIVE.	
BETHUNE	14th		In billets. O C to NOYELLES & back to take over from ~~#~~ 509th London Field Co. 6th Div in HOHENZOLLERN Sector. Frost at night	
NOYELLES -LEZ-VERMELLES	15th		Co with transport by march route arriving 12.30 p.m. Into same ~~[illegible]~~ billets as before (in Oct, Nov, Dec 1916). Mild.	
"	16th		Officers round trenches to see work in progress. Cold.	
"	17th		-Do- Work started at night. A lot of work has been done on revetting of Communication Trenches but much remains. Trenches where not revetted will fall in when thaw sets in as it shows signs of doing.	
	18th		Work in full swing, mainly on C.T.'s. Wet. Trenches are falling in badly	
	19th		-do-	
	20th		Steady rain. C.R.E. round line with O.C. Co.	

8353 Wt. W2544/1454 700,000 5/15 D. D. & L. A.D.S.S./Forms/C. 2118.

Instructions regarding War Diaries and Intelligence Summaries are contained in F. S. Regs., Part II. and the Staff Manual respectively. Title pages will be prepared in manuscript.

WAR DIARY

~~or~~

~~INTELLIGENCE SUMMARY.~~

(Erase heading not required.)

Army Form C. 2118.

98th Field Co — Feb 1917 contd

Place	Date	Hour	Summary of Events and Information	Remarks and references to Appendices
NOYELLES-LEZ-VERMELLES	Feb 21st to 27th		Inter Battalion Relief in trenches much delayed by very bad state of trenches which have fallen in badly. From now on about 600 men are employed daily in clearing mud out of communication trenches. Fortunately the days are misty up to 25th Feb and much traffic can go on above ground. Only two out of the four main communication trenches behind the RESERVE Line are being dealt with, the others being temporarily abandoned. By 27th Feb (relief day) two CTs are fairly passable up to Reserve Line & thence to front four CTs are good. Weather fortunately fine. 25th & 26th Feb sunny & warm.	
	28th		110th Inf Bde take over half the 62nd Bde front, on their right. OC round part of new area to see work in hand. Misty	
			No battle casualties during month.	
			[signature] Maj RE O.C. 98 Field Co.	

Vol 19

Confidential

War Diary

of

98th Field Co R. E.

March 1st – 31st 1917

Vol XIX

Instructions regarding War Diaries and Intelligence Summaries are contained in F. S. Regs., Part II. and the Staff Manual respectively. Title pages will be prepared in manuscript.

WAR DIARY
or
INTELLIGENCE SUMMARY.
(Erase heading not required.)

98th Field Coy Mar. 1917.

98th Field Co RE

Army Form C. 2118.

Place	Date	Hour	Summary of Events and Information	Remarks and references to Appendices
NOYELLES-LES-VERMELLES	Mar. 1st to 4th		About 600 men are employed daily in clearing mud & falls out of communication trenches and revetting trenches above the RESERVE LINE weather fair	
	5th		Inter Battalion Relief	
	6th		Major Coachman went to act as CRE Capt. Dakin took over command of the Coy on the 7th	
	to		Work continued on C.T.s keeping them clear and revetting as much as possible	
			18 men being trained with Bangalore Torpedos and the use of Mobile charges in conjunction with the Infantry. Frosty weather again	
	9th			
	10th		Thaw set in again trenches very bad with mud all working parties clearing main Communication trench of mud and falls due to thaw	
	11th		Inter Battalion Relief some trenches in a very bad state	
	to		Work continued on C.T.s which are now fairly good by the 15th	
	15th			
	16th	5.0am	German trenches raided on DIAMOND POINT G5d 20 35. Two torpedos were blown on the right clearing a gap of 30 feet, the right party were stopped by 2nd belt of wire, a 4 foot gap was cut in this but there was no time left to enter German trenches. On the left the wire had been cut by the Artillery, no torpedos being used. The German trenches were entered. Sappers going with the Infantry and three dugout entrances were blown in and a Concrete Machine Gun Emplacement blown up by mobile charges. We had one casualty L/Cpl Bambrick being wounded.	
	17th		Inter Battalion Relief.	

8353 Wt. W2544/1454 700,000 5/15 D. D. & L. A.D.S.S./Forms/C. 2118.

Army Form C. 2118.

Instructions regarding War Diaries and Intelligence Summaries are contained in F. S. Regs., Part II. and the Staff Manual respectively. Title pages will be prepared in manuscript.

WAR DIARY
or
~~INTELLIGENCE SUMMARY.~~

98th Field Co (Erase heading not required.) March 1917.

Place	Date	Hour	Summary of Events and Information	Remarks and references to Appendices
NOYELLES -LEZ-VERMELLES	March 18th–27		Work on C.T's continued and by the end of the period these were fairly well cleared. The RESERVE line between GORDON alley and O.B.1 was realigned and the new portion was revetted throughout	
"	March 27th		Work on Right half of HOHENZOLLERN Sector handed over to 459th Field Co 6th Divn, left half to 432nd Field Co 66th Divn.	
"	28th		Mounted portion of Co (+ cyclists) marched to CAMBLAIN l'ABBÉ.	
"	29th	8.30 a.m	Dismounted portion of Co (+ attached Infantry) in busses to LARBRET Station. Thence marched to billets in POMMIER. Mounted portion marched to POMMIER. Wet	
POMMIER	30th		Rest. Major COUCHMAN rejoined Co.	
"	31st		Cleaning up camp & repairs to billets.	

31.3.17

[signature] Major RE
O.C. 98th F. Co.

Instructions regarding War Diaries and Intelligence Summaries are contained in F. S. Regs., Part II. and the Staff Manual respectively. Title pages will be prepared in manuscript.

WAR DIARY
~~or~~
~~INTELLIGENCE~~ SUMMARY.
(Erase heading not required.)

Army Form C. 2118.

98th Field Coy RE

98th Field Co — April 1917 — Vol 20

Place	Date	Hour	Summary of Events and Information	Remarks and references to Appendices
POMMIER	April 1st–3rd		Co. principally employed on improving horse lines & road. Training of officers & senior N.C.Os. in compass marching.	
"	4th	9 a.m.	Co less some transport marched to HAMELINCOURT. Arrived 2.30 p.m. Spent rest of day in improvising bivouacs in ruins of village. Rain & cold	
HAMELIN-COURT	5th		Co. principally employed on clearing roads in village, improving bivouacs and sinking a well. Also started making huts for 110th Bde H.Q. in the village.	
"	6th		Work continued. Started clearing trees across road ~~E of HAM~~ to ST. LEGER.	
"	7th		– do – as on 6th. Also started deviation round crater blown at cross roads on ST LEGER road.	
"	8th		– do – as on 7th. Also started advanced Bde H.Q. 2 miles E of HAMELINCOURT ~~village~~ in railway cutting. This work was cancelled the same evening & only a small Report centre is required. Rest of transport etc left at POMMIER marched to HAMELINCOURT.	
"	9th		– do – as on 8th. Completed clearing of trees & deviation round crater today. 64th Inf Bde attacked enemy trenches in afternoon. No special work assigned to Co.	
"	10th		Work continued. Started deviation round another crater on ST LEGER road E of JUDAS FARM.	
"	11th–14th		Continued work on MAISON ROUGE – CROISILLES road. Road surface is generally bad & requires large quantity of road metal.	

8353 Wt. W2544/1454 700,000 5/15 D. D. & L. A.D.S.S./Forms/C. 2118.

Instructions regarding War Diaries and Intelligence Summaries are contained in F. S. Regs., Part II. and the Staff Manual respectively. Title pages will be prepared in manuscript.

WAR DIARY

~~or~~ ~~INTELLIGENCE SUMMARY.~~

(Erase heading not required.)

98th Field Co — April 1917.

Army Form C. 2118.

Place	Date	Hour	Summary of Events and Information	Remarks and references to Appendices
BAILLEUL-MONT	15th		Whole Co marched ~~to B~~ from HAMELINCOURT 11 a.m. Cold & wet. Into R.E. camp. Good huts & covered horse standings.	
"	16th–23rd		Overhauling equipment, practising with Service Trestle & other light work. Worked on roads in village.	
BOIRY-ST-RICTRUDE	24th		Left Bailleulmont 7.30 a.m. Into bivouac. Fine	
"	25th		In bivouac. Rest	
" "	26th		Marched 9.0 a.m. arrived JUDAS FARM about ¾ mile W. of ST LEGER. Co employed rest of day in making shelter for themselves.	
JUDAS FARM	27th		No. 1 Section worked on crater diversions, No. 3 Section started new Bde H.Q. in a sunken road. No. 2 & 4 section worked during night on strong points along a defensive line running just E of ST LEGER & thence N.N.E. along reverse slope of a ridge. No. 3 Secn also started sinking wells in CROISILLES & ST LEGER.	
"	28th		3 Sections on strong points. No. 3 Secn as above. 1 Co of Pioneer Bn also on strong points	
"	29th		as on 28th without Pioneer Co. Weather very fine & hot, the first this year.	
"	30th		as on 29th. Pioneer Co working today on wire round & between the strong points. Very fine & warm.	
			a/Cpl McGRATH. E was awarded a bar to Military Medal for his work during the raid in the HOHENZOLLERN Sector on March 16th. He successfully exploded a Bangalore torpedo destroying one belt of enemy wire & with Lance Corporal PORTER of the Co cut a gap through a second belt with wirecutters.	
			No battle casualties up to noon 30th	
			Strength at beginning of month 207, at end 214	
			K. [signature] Major R.E. O.C. 98th F. Co	[initials]
			30.4.17	

#353 Wt. W2544/1454 700,000 5/15 D. D. & L. A.D.S.S./Forms/C. 2118.

Vol 21

CONFIDENTIAL

WAR DIARY

OF

98TH FIELD COMPANY RE

FROM 1st MAY 1917. to 31st MAY 1917.

VOLUME. 21.

Army Form C. 2118.

Instructions regarding War Diaries and Intelligence Summaries are contained in F. S. Regs., Part II. and the Staff Manual respectively. Title pages will be prepared in manuscript.

WAR DIARY
or
~~INTELLIGENCE~~ SUMMARY.

(Erase heading not required.)

98th Field Co RE

98th Field Co R.E.

May 1917.

Place	Date	Hour	Summary of Events and Information	Remarks and references to Appendices
			1/20000 Sheet 51 B. S.W.	
JUDAS FARM near ST. LEGER	May 1st		Completed Posts 1 to 5 along defensive line running N from E. edge of ST LEGER. Work on new wells in ST LEGER & CROISILLES stopped temporarily. During night cleared a track for horse transport through Eastern outskirts of CROISILLES. CRE issued operation order for R.E. work during attack on May 3rd. Very fine.	
	2nd		Made up loads of RE stores to be carried to sites of strong points to be made round FONTAINE-LEZ-CROISILLES. Made up mobile charges (20 lbs ammonal) for 110th Inf Bde. a few other light jobs. Very fine. Reconnoitred route to assembly position.	
	3rd	4.30 a.m	Marched to assembly position in T. 4. b & remained there until 2.15 a.m, 4th. O C remained at 110th Inf Bde H. Q in HINDENBURG Support line all day. At 10.30 p.m orders issued for 100 Infantry attached to the Co to move up and improve our old front line. No casualties. Very fine	
	4th		Co returned to billets 4.0 a.m, attached Infantry 6.0 a.m. Co moved out 7.30 p.m and wired & made good, German C.T. between HINDENBURG front & support line in T. 6. a. Used pack horses for carrying barbed wire to site, the first time this has been used in France by this Co. Very fine. Reconnoitred sites for strong posts E & N.E of CROISILLES	
	5th		Returned to billets 4.0. a.m. Co moved out 8.0 p.m & started 3 strong posts round CROISILLES to NE & E. Corp COTTEE, Sapper TUCKER, CLAYTON, & HURCOMBE and 1 attached Infantry private wounded, mostly very slight.	
	6th		Returned to billets 3.30 a.m. Moved out 8.15 p.m & completed the 3 strong posts C_3, C_4 & C_5 & wired along whole length. about 2700 yards of wire put out in 2 nights. Sapper DARNTON wounded.	

$353 Wt. W2544/1454 700,000 5/15 D. D. & L. A.D.S.S./Forms/C. 2118.

Instructions regarding War Diaries and Intelligence Summaries are contained in F. S. Regs., Part II. and the Staff Manual respectively. Title pages will be prepared in manuscript.

WAR DIARY

~~or~~

~~INTELLIGENCE SUMMARY.~~

(Erase heading not required.)

Army Form C. 2118.

98th Field Co RE

May 1917.

Place	Date	Hour	Summary of Events and Information	Remarks and references to Appendices
			Sheet 1/20000 51 B S.W.	
JUDAS FARM	7th		Returned to billets 3.30 a.m. Restarted work on new wells in CROISILLES & ST LEGER at night. ~~B~~ Remainder of Co resting. Very fine.	
	8th		CROISILLES well finished; this is 7'6" square inside casing, 14'6" deep to bottom, 3' to water level. Found water in ST LEGER well at 18'6". Dumped wire & pickets at Strong posts 1 to 7 & C1 to C5 vide sketch. Commenced filling in crater on CROISILLES-FONTAINE Road. This is 50 ft across & 18 ft deep. Wet.	
			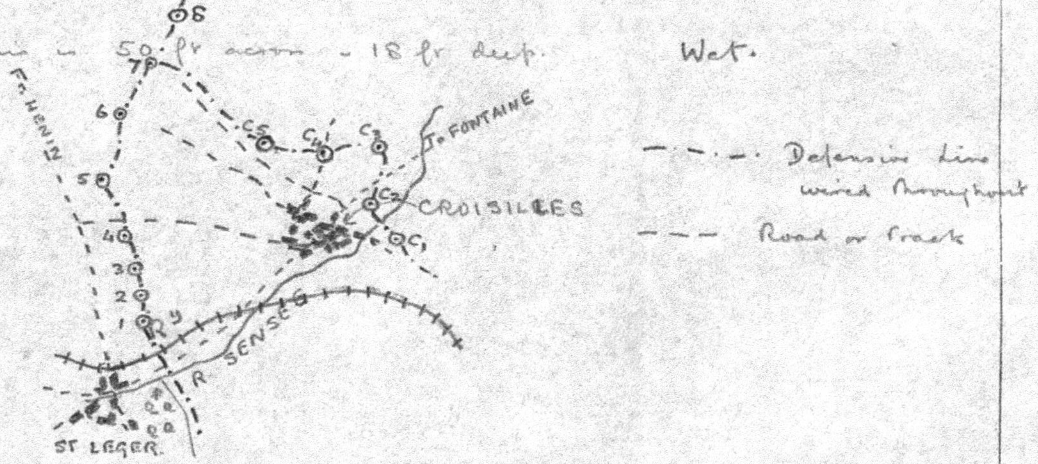	
	9th		Continued on well in ST LEGER & crater on CROISILLES-FONTAINE Road. Other minor jobs in hand.	
	10th		As on 9th. In addition worked on CROISILLES-HENIN Road & fixed small shelter in Strong post 5 & 8. ~~Crater on CROISILLES~~	
	11th		As on 10th. Crater on CROISILLES-FONTAINE road filled in flush with road with earth.	

#353 Wt. W2544/1454 700,000 5/15 D. D. & L. A.D.S.S./Forms/C. 2118.

Army Form C. 2118.

WAR DIARY
or
~~INTELLIGENCE SUMMARY.~~
(*Erase heading not required.*)

Instructions regarding War Diaries and Intelligence Summaries are contained in F. S. Regs., Part II. and the Staff Manual respectively. Title pages will be prepared in manuscript.

98th Field Co — May 1917.

Place	Date	Hour	Summary of Events and Information	Remarks and references to Appendices
JUDAS. Fme.	11th contd.		After earth has settled roadway will be made. Sappers NETHERTON, GOSS, REECE & 1 attached Infy wounded at crater, the two latter very slight.	
"	12th	7.30 a.m	Marched to BIENVILLIERS-AU-BOIS on relief by 222nd Field Co 33rd Div. Very hot	
BIENVILLERS -AU-BOIS	13th		Co. in rest. Work mainly drill & musketry. Inter company sports at RANSART 20th May.	
	—		Result. 21st Sig. Co 39 points, 98th Fd Co 27, 97th Fd Co 23, 126th Fd Co 5 points. Lance Cpl	
			BUTTON to England 15th for commission in Infy.	
	21st		Co inspected by the CRE at RANSART	
	23rd		Co inspected by GOC 21st Div	
	26th		Co transport inspected by OC 21st Div. Train	
	27th 30th		Work mainly drill & musketry one section working on Hutting at HUMBERCAMP	
	31st	5.0am	Marched to HAMBLINCOURT & took over from the 11th Field Coy 38th Div Very hot.	

1-6-17

E. W. Walker Capt RE
O/C 98th Fd Cy RE

A6945 Wt. W11422/M1160 350,000 12/16 D. D. & L. Forms/C./2118/14.

CONFIDENTIAL

Vol 22

WAR. DIARY.

OF

98th Field Coy. R.E.

FROM. 1st June 1917. TO. 30th June 1917.

VOLUME. 22.

98th Field Coy RE

Army Form C. 2118.

Instructions regarding War Diaries and Intelligence Summaries are contained in F. S. Regs., Part II. and the Staff Manual respectively. Title pages will be prepared in manuscript.

WAR DIARY
or
~~INTELLIGENCE SUMMARY.~~

(Erase heading not required.)

98th Field Co. June 1917

Place	Date	Hour	Summary of Events and Information	Remarks and references to Appendices
HAMELINCOURT	June 1st		During night 1st/2nd 1 Section with 300 Infy dug close support line (LINCOLN Trench) between ~~the~~ FACTORY & NELLY Avenues. Rest of Co worked on water points in MOYENNEVILLE & HAMELINCOURT & in camp.	
	2nd		Completed LINCOLN Trench during night. Other work as before. Made concertina barbed wire. 200 Infy under our supervision extended FACTORY avenue westward. Sapper DRANSFIELD wounded.	
	3rd		Continued work on FACTORY Avenue. Other work as ~~usual~~ before. Started assisting Infy to make latrine seats etc in Brigade camp MOYENNEVILLE.	
	4th		as on 3rd. Started bath house for Reserve Bde in MOYENNEVILLE	
	5th & 6th		as on 4th	
	7th		Work as before. Nearly all Co transport, including three G.S. wagons from A.S.C which have been lent to the Co while in the line, with cyclists employed in salving old German knife rests from surrounding country, there being a sudden & urgent demand for these in front line.	
	8th		as on 6th.	
	9th		as on 8th. Half Section started erecting cookhouses at site of new Divisional	

Instructions regarding War Diaries and Intelligence Summaries are contained in F. S. Regs., Part II. and the Staff Manual respectively. Title pages will be prepared in manuscript.

Army Form C. 2118.

WAR DIARY

~~or~~

~~INTELLIGENCE SUMMARY.~~

(Erase heading not required.)

98th Field Co R.E. June 1917

Place	Date	Hour	Summary of Events and Information	Remarks and references to Appendices
HAMELINCOURT	June 10th		Work on Communication Trenches (FACTORY, NELLY & JANET avenues) continued. 1 Section of Co has been working throughout on these, Lieut HEWIN & Lieut McLAREN of the Co detailed to assist Infantry in Trench work in Right Sector now held by 110th Inf Bde (to which 98th Co is normally affiliated)	
	11th		Lieut HEPBURN of the Co detailed to assist R.A in their construction work. This officer lives with R.A. H.Q. & has 3 NCOs & 3 Sappers from the Co to help the R.A.	
	12th		22 huts (VII Corps pattern) allotted for Reserve Bde Camp, MOYENNEVILLE. 1 Section started erection of these. Other work as usual.	
	13th		Nothing to report.	
	14th		Urgent demand for concertina barbed wire & extra men put on to this. 150 coils sent to ST LEGER dump.	
	15th		200 coils concertina wire made & sent to ST LEGER.	
	16th		110th Inf Bde attacked TUNNEL Trench at 3.10 a.m. a/Cpl McGRATH and 4 Sappers with mobile charges went over with Right Bn in order to supervise the blocking of the tunnel under this trench. This party did nothing as attack failed	

A6945 Wt. W11422/M1160 350,000 12/16 D. D. & L. Forms/C./2118/14.

Instructions regarding War Diaries and Intelligence Summaries are contained in F. S. Regs., Part II. and the Staff Manual respectively. Title pages will be prepared in manuscript.

WAR DIARY
or
~~INTELLIGENCE SUMMARY.~~

(Erase heading not required.)

Army Form C. 2118.

98th Field Co R.E. — June 1917.

Place	Date	Hour	Summary of Events and Information	Remarks and references to Appendices
	June		~~Lines laid before the attack Lieuts Gregson & Campbell set out guiding tapes for the~~ attacking infantry Lieut Gregson wounded.	
HAMELINCOURT	16th cont'd		& Capt. McGRATH was killed. O.C. with 2 officers & about 60 men of Co left camp 1.0 a.m. being detailed for various work in ~~[illegible]~~ Tunnel Trench. This could not be carried out & party remained in a trench until 5 p.m. without casualties. Weather very hot as it has been throughout except for occasional thunder showers.	
"	17th } 18th } 19th		Nothing to report. Demand for concertina wire slackened. 22 huts completed (vide entry on 12th). Packing wagons & cleaning up.	
"	20th		Marched 5.0 a.m. arrived RANSART 7.15 a.m. & took over billets of 212th Fd Co, 33rd Div. who relieve us at HAMELINCOURT. Major COUCHMAN acts as CRE, Capt DAKIN acts as O.C. 98th Co.	
RANSART	21st – 29th		Co in rest. Some men employed throughout the period in completing new Div. H.Q. at MOYENNEVILLE. Considerable amount of salvage done in old front line system mainly trench boards. Other work mainly drill & odd jobs. A 2 day course in elementary Mil. Engineering for Infantry officers & N.C.O's from 110th Inf Bde held at RANSART on 25th & 26th.	
	30		Packing wagons and cleaning up.	

E. C. Dakin Capt. R.E.
OC 98th Fd Coy RE

A6945 Wt. W11422/M1160 350,000 12/16 D. D. & L. Forms/C./2118/14.

CONFIDENTIAL

WAR DIARY

Vol 23

OF

98TH FIELD COMPANY R.E.

FROM 1ST JULY 1917 TO 31ST JULY 1917

VOLUME 23.

98TH
FIELD COMPANY,
R.E.
No. C/1963
Date 1-8-17

98th Field Coy R.E.

Army Form C. 2118.

Instructions regarding War Diaries and Intelligence Summaries are contained in F. S. Regs., Part II. and the Staff Manual respectively. Title pages will be prepared in manuscript.

WAR DIARY
or
~~INTELLIGENCE SUMMARY.~~
(Erase heading not required.)

98th Field Coy R.E. July 1917.

Place	Date	Hour	Summary of Events and Information	Remarks and references to Appendices
RANSART	1.		Marched 7-0 am arrived HAMELINCOURT 9-15am took over billets of 212 Fd Coy 33rd Div. Major Coachman appointed CRE 39th Div & to be T/Lt Col. Auth XVII Corps C/1000 of 1/7/17	
HAMELINCOURT	2nd		A/Capt C.H.V. Dakin assumed command of the 98th Fd Coy Auth. A.G. GHQ A22358/788 of 29/6/17	
	5th		All work in back area 1 Secn completing Div. HQ Camp 1 Secn working on new water point MOYENNEVILLE 2 Secs working in Camp & making Concertina wire, also cleaning out 3 wells in HAMLINCOURT.	
	6th to 9th		No 2 Secn with 50 attd Inf proceeded to SHAFT TRENCH billeting in the tunnel, and became attached to the 97th Field Coy for work. 2Lt ~~[illegible]~~ WOMERSLEY joined the Coy. Remainder of the Coy work as on the 5th	
	10th & 11th		As on 6th Work started on workshop at CRE dump BOYELLES	
	12th		As on 10th Div. HQ mess & camp finished.	
	15th		As on 12th Church parade at 5.30 pm.	
	16th to 27th		No 3 Sec relieved No 2 Sec in the trenches. Work continued on RE Dump BOYELLES & on WATER POINTS in MOYENNEVILLE	
	28th		Marched 9.0am arrived BOIRY BECQUERELLE 10.15am took over billets of 97th Fd Coy RE and all trench work.	
		night 28/29.	One N.C.O. & 2 Sapr went with a raiding party to cut the wire with	

A6945 Wt. W11422/M1160 350,000 12/16 D. D. & L. Forms/C./2118/14.

Army Form C. 2118.

WAR DIARY
or
~~INTELLIGENCE SUMMARY.~~
(Erase heading not required.)

Instructions regarding War Diaries and Intelligence Summaries are contained in F. S. Regs., Part II. and the Staff Manual respectively. Title pages will be prepared in manuscript.

98th Field Coy — July 1917

Place	Date	Hour	Summary of Events and Information	Remarks and references to Appendices
BOIRY BECQUERELLE	Night	28/29	Bangalore torpedoes, but they were not used	
	29th to 30		Work in trenches, revetting, clearing and making dugouts. One Section of 97th Fd Coy attached for work in trenches	
	Night	30/31	6 Sappers ~~under~~ went out with a raiding party to destroy wire with Bangalore torpedo. the torpedoes were not needed.	
	31		Work as usual in trenches, O.C. went round the HINDENBURG LINE, with the Corps Water Engineer to look at a proposed water scheme	

[signature] Major RE
OC 98 Fd Coy RE
31-7-17

CONFIDENTIAL

Vol 24

WAR DIARY

OF

98TH FIELD Co RE

FROM 1ST AUGUST 1917 TO 31ST AUGUST 1917

VOLUME 24

98TH FIELD COMPANY, R.E.
No. C/2221.
Date

Instructions regarding War Diaries and Intelligence Summaries are contained in F. S. Regs., Part II. and the Staff Manual respectively. Title pages will be prepared in manuscript.

WAR DIARY
or
~~INTELLIGENCE SUMMARY.~~
(*Erase heading not required.*)

Army Form C. 2118.

98th Field Coy RE — August 1917

Place	Date	Hour	Summary of Events and Information	Remarks and references to Appendices
BOIRY BECQUERELLE	1st to 2nd		Work in trenches revetting & trenchboarding one section from the 97th Fd Coy attached for work	
	3rd		On on 1st night of 3rd/4th blew up a tank near TANK TRENCH this to 300 lbs of explosive and was completely destroyed	
	4th to 8th		Owing to Div: ~~handing~~ going to hand over the line north of PUG LANE to 50 Div. all work on trenches north of PUG LANE was stopped, and all sections worked on PUG LANE - CLAW TR and SHAFT & HIND TRENCHES getting these trenches in good order by the 8th	
St LEGER	9th		HQs with 2 & 3 Sections (attd sec: 97th Coy) moved to billets of 528 Fd Coy in St LEGER.	
			No 1 Sec moved into tunnel in SHAFT Tr. No 4 Sec remained at BOIRY-BECQUERELLE, working trenches from NELLY Av to SENSEE RIVER taken over from 126 Coy	
	10th		No 1 Sec started working chambers for billets in the tunnel in SHAFT TR. No 4 continued working trenches North of SENSEE RIVER. No 2 & 3 Secs took over work in LUMP LANE & HIND Tr South of SENSEE RIVER. Lt G.A. Gregson rejoined the Coy.	
	11th to 12th		Work on trenches continued	

A6945 Wt. W11422/M1160 350,000 12/16 D. D. & L. Forms/C./2118/14.

Army Form C. 2118.

Instructions regarding War Diaries and Intelligence Summaries are contained in F. S. Regs., Part II. and the Staff Manual respectively. Title pages will be prepared in manuscript.

WAR DIARY
or
INTELLIGENCE SUMMARY.
(*Erase heading not required.*)

98th Fd Coy R.E. — August

Place	Date	Hour	Summary of Events and Information	Remarks and references to Appendices
ST. LEGER	14th to 17th		30 Officers + NCO's of 9th Batt. Leic. Regt. did revetting etc as a class under RE. supervision on posts C_2 + C_3. Work on trenches continued. No 2 section put an inverted siphon under HIND TRENCH where the SENSEE RIVER crossed it. No. 1 section started grading + draining a trench tramway track on the left battalion sector. 25 men of No 1 sec. + its attached infantry moved from BOIRY BECQUERELLE to ST. LEGER. (17th)	
	17th		Rest day. Men had baths.	
	18th to 21st		Work on trenches continued. No. 1 Sec. continued tramway on left sector + dug out ROYAL DUMP on the right sector.	
	22nd		Battalion relief. Work on left sector + tunnel dugout continued. No. 1 Sec. continued work on ROYAL DUMP. Remainder of Coy. started work on winter billets in ST. LEGER.	
	23rd to 25th		Work continued. Tunnel dugout completed with bunked accommodation for 45 men. Tramway continued.	
	26th		Rest day. Cleaning up. Work handed over to 155th Fd. Co. Billets handed over to 156th Fd. Co.	
	27th		Mounted portion of Coy. + cyclists moved to FOSSEUX by road. Dismounted portion of Coy. + attached infantry moved by light railway from ST. LEGER to BEAUMETZ and marched into hut camp at FOSSEUX from BEAUMETZ.	

A6945 Wt. W11422/M1160 350,000 12/16 D. D. & L. Forms/C./2118/14.

Army Form C. 2118.

WAR DIARY
or
~~INTELLIGENCE~~ ~~SUMMARY~~.
(Erase heading not required.)

Instructions regarding War Diaries and Intelligence Summaries are contained in F. S. Regs., Part II, and the Staff Manual respectively. Title pages will be prepared in manuscript.

98th F Coy RE   August

Place	Date	Hour	Summary of Events and Information	Remarks and references to Appendices
FOSSEUX	28th to 31st		Training. Attached infantry rejoined battalions on 29th	
			[signature] Major RE OC 98 F Coy RE	

A6945 Wt. W11422/M1160 350,000 12/16 D. D. & L. Forms/C./2118/14.

CONFIDENTIAL

WAR DIARY

OF

98TH FIELD COMPANY R.E.

Vol 25

FROM 1ST SEPT. 1917 TO 30TH SEPT 1917.

VOL. 25

FIELD COMPANY, R.E.
D/2579
Date........

Army Form C. 2118.

Instructions regarding War Diaries and Intelligence Summaries are contained in F. S. Regs., Part II. and the Staff Manual respectively. Title pages will be prepared in manuscript.

WAR DIARY
or
~~INTELLIGENCE SUMMARY.~~
(Erase heading not required.)

98th Field Coy RE — September

Place	Date	Hour	Summary of Events and Information	Remarks and references to Appendices
FOSSEUX	1st-5th		Training	
	6th		Entrained at AUBIGNY proceeded to HOPOUTRE marched to RIDGE WOOD	
			hutting in NISSEN HUTS	
	7th		Marched to MILLEKRUIS camped under canvas	
			Worked on Horse standings and Hutting for CRE X Corps	
	18th & 19th		6 men worked for MG Coy making shelters. One Section worked on roads to	
			Gun emplacements on the OBSERVATORY RIDGE	
	18th & 29th		One Section & transport marched to ABEELE and worked on Hutting	
			Remainder of the Coy worked on Horse standings & huts	
	30th		Dismounted men of the Coy moved to dugouts in the bank of ZILLEBEKE LAKE	
			Transport & HdQrs remained at MILLEKRUIS. The section working on hutting at ABEELE	
			rejoined the Coy	

[signature] Major RE
OC 98th Fd Coy RE

A6945 Wt. W11422/M1160 350,000 12/16 D. D. & L. Forms/C./2118/14.

Vol 26

— CONFIDENTIAL —

WAR DIARY

OF

98TH FIELD COMPANY RE

FROM. 1ST OCT. 1917 — TO 31ST OCT. 1917

VOLUME 26.

98TH
FIELD COMPANY.
R.E.
No. D/2724
Date 2-11-17.

Instructions regarding War Diaries and Intelligence Summaries are contained in F. S. Regs., Part II. and the Staff Manual respectively. Title pages will be prepared in manuscript.

WAR DIARY
or
~~INTELLIGENCE SUMMARY.~~ OCTOBER

98th Field Coy RE (*Erase heading not required.*)

Army Form C. 2118.

Place	Date	Hour	Summary of Events and Information	Remarks and references to Appendices
ZILLEBEKE LAKE	1st		One Section worked on wells in POLYGONE WOOD. Two sections worked on making	
	to		and marking tracks from CLAPHAM JUNCTION through GLENCORSE & POLYGONE	
	3rd		wood to the front line. One section remained in Camp improving billets	
			and making [illegible] board. 140 Infantry were attached to the Coy for work on	
			the 1st – Lt Hewin was wounded on the 3rd. On the 3rd Coy moved to dugouts in R[?] bank near ZILLEBEKE LAKE	
	4th		The night of 3/4th & day of the 4th Coy rested in billets. OC remained at 62 Inf Bde HQrs	
	4th	9.0pm	Three sections and their attached Inf moved up to the front line and succeeded in	
			digging three strong points near JUDGE TRENCH the line of the 1st objective	
			which was about 200 yds behind the new front line. One of the strong points	
			was wired by a Coy of Pioneers of 14th North Fus. Coy arrived back in billets at	
	5th		7.0 am on 5th. The Coy had 20 casualties. – Horse lines moved to Camp near SCOTTISH WOOD.	
	5th	6.0pm	Four sections with attached Inf & two Coys of 14th North Fus (Pio) went to front line	
			3 sections revetted with A frames the fire bays of the strong points dug the	
			night before. One section dug a new strong on the Rt flank. The Pioneers wired	
			all strong points and all the right flank (see sketch)	
	6th	8.0am	Coy arrived back into new ~~billets~~ Camp next SCOTTISH WOOD	

A6945 Wt. W11422/M1160 350,000 12/16 D. D. & L. Forms/C./2118/14.

Instructions regarding War Diaries and Intelligence Summaries are contained in F. S. Regs., Part II. and the Staff Manual respectively. Title pages will be prepared in manuscript.

WAR DIARY
or
~~INTELLIGENCE SUMMARY.~~
(*Erase heading not required.*)

98th Field Coy RE — OCTOBER

Army Form C. 2118.

Place	Date	Hour	Summary of Events and Information	Remarks and references to Appendices
	6th		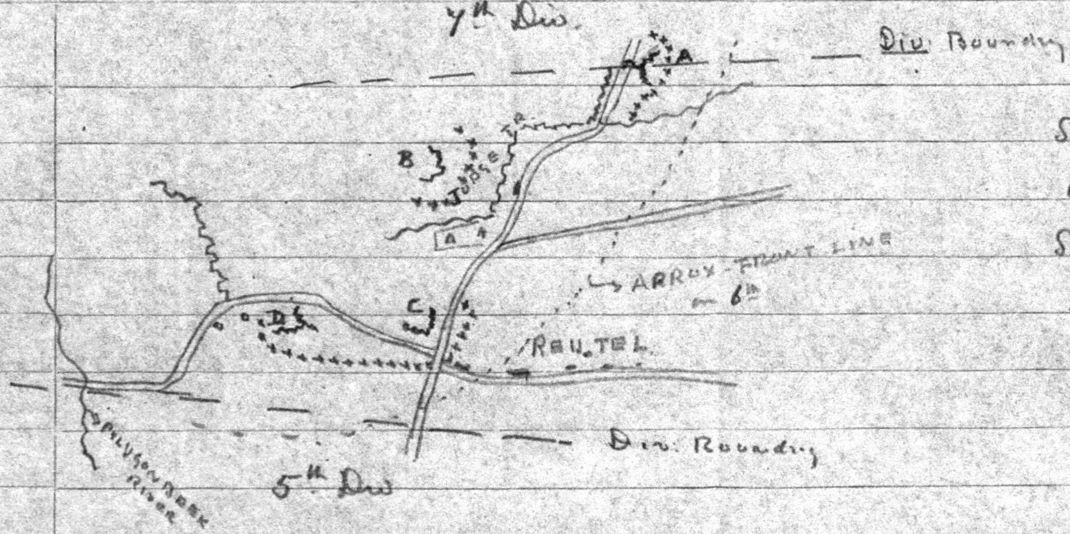 Strong point A.B.C dug on night of 4/5th + point A wired as shown. Strong points A.B.C revetted, point D dug. Points B.C.D wired as shown xxxx on night of 6th/7th	
	7th		Coy Rested. One Section on night 7/8th went as loading party with wagons taking planks for road near GLENCORSE wood	
	8th & 10		Two Sections worked on new plank road west of GLENCORSE wood. One section acting as loading party to wagons at night. One section resting, Lt Moss and attached Inf returned to their B^ns on the 9th	
	11th		Coy and Transport moved to Huts at the Bombing School BOESCHEPPE	
	12th		Coy rested	

A6945 Wt. W11422/M1160 350,000 12/16 D. D. & L. Forms/C./2118/14.

Army Form C. 2118.

Instructions regarding War Diaries and Intelligence Summaries are contained in F. S. Regs., Part II. and the Staff Manual respectively. Title pages will be prepared in manuscript.

WAR DIARY
or
INTELLIGENCE SUMMARY.
(Erase heading not required.)

98th Fd Coy RE — OCTOBER

Place	Date	Hour	Summary of Events and Information	Remarks and references to Appendices
BOESCHEPPE	13th		Coy had baths and started work on Huts for X Corps School	
	14th to 16		Coy worked on Hut site of X Corps School	
	17		Coy moved to Signal School	
	20		Continued work on School	
	21st		Coy Rested	
	22		Coy & transport moved to Huts in RIDGE WOOD	
	23rd		3 Section worked in back area building drying Huts for batt Camps and improving Div HQs Camp. One section worked on Coy Camp. 100 ~~men~~ Inf under 2 Lt Moon were attached for work	
	23 to 30		Continued work on Div HQ + Back area camps	
	31st		Took over work in the line from 126 Fd Coy RE – Two section with Att Inf repairing and extending a duck board track through POLYGONE wood to the front line	
			Awards. Military Medal No 46630 2/Cpl King C.C.; No 80390 Dr L/Cpl Goy H. X Corps RO 1769, 17/10/17	
			Military Cross. Capt a/Major E L V Dakin – Lieut F Hewson X Corps RO a/22 23.10.17	
			Military Medal Sgt Watson J X Corps RO a/22 23.10.17	

E L V Dakin Major RE
OC 98 Fd Coy RE

A6945 Wt. W11422/M1160 350,000 12/16 D. D. & L. Forms/C./2118/14.

CONFIDENTIAL

Vol 27

WAR DIARY

OF

98TH FIELD Coy RE

FROM 1ST NOV 1917 TO 30TH NOV 1917

VOLUME 26

98TH
FIELD COMPANY,
R.E.
No. D/2978
Date

Instructions regarding War Diaries and Intelligence Summaries are contained in F. S. Regs., Part II. and the Staff Manual respectively. Title pages will be prepared in manuscript.

98th Fd Coy RE

WAR DIARY
or
~~INTELLIGENCE SUMMARY.~~
(Erase heading not required.)

NOVEMBER

Army Form C. 2118.

Place	Date	Hour	Summary of Events and Information	Remarks and references to Appendices
RIDGE WOOD	1st to 14th		Coy worked on ~~dr~~ duckboard tracks through GLENCORSE + POLYGON WOOD to front line. Two Sections with their attd Inf working alternate days. 5 OR killed 2 OR wounded in this period	
	15th		Coy Relieved by the 1st ANZAC Fd Coy RE. and all work taken over by them. Coy Rested	
BUSSEBOME	16th		Coy & transport moved to Camp at BUSSEBOME.	
	17th		Coy Rested.	
DOULIEU	18th		Coy & transport marched to billets at DOULIEU -	
	19th		Coy Rested	
OBLINGHEM	20		Coy & transport marched to billets at OBLINGHEM	
COUPIGNY	21st to 24		" " " " " COUPIGNY	
			Coy rested and trained in drill + musketry	
BAJUS	25		Coy & transport marched to Billets at BAJUS	
	26 to 29		Coy in training including, drill, Pontoon & trestle bridging	
	30	7-30	Coy marched from BAJUS to SAVY + entrained 11-30A for TINCOURT. Transport moved by road at 8-30 to ARRAS.	

C W Oakes Major RE
OC 98th Fd Coy RE

A6945 Wt. W11422/M1160 350,000 12/16 D. D. & L. Forms/C./2118/14.

Vol 28

CONFIDENTIAL

OF

98TH FIELD COMPANY RE

FROM 1ST DEC. 1917

TO 31ST DEC. 1917

VOLUME 27.

98TH FIELD COMPANY, R.E.
No. 8/3258
Date 13.1.18.

Instructions regarding War Diaries and Intelligence Summaries are contained in F. S. Regs., Part II. and the Staff Manual respectively. Title pages will be prepared in manuscript.

WAR DIARY
or
INTELLIGENCE SUMMARY.
(Erase heading not required.)

Army Form C. 2118.

Place	Date	Hour	Summary of Events and Information	Remarks and references to Appendices
near QUISANTS	1.12.17		Transport arrived 4 am. Left again at 9 am. & marched to BAPAUME where it bivouacked for the night. Dismounted portion of Coy. arrived TINCOURT & was billeted in huts.	
BAPAUME	2.12.17 to 5.12.17		Transport marched to TINCOURT. Dismounted portion of Coy. rested. Whole Coy. rested till 5th.12.17.	
TINCOURT	5.12.17		Nos 2 & 4 sections moved up to forward dugout billets in the railway near EPEHY	
	7.12.17		100 infantry joined the forward sections for work. Work done was putting in shelters in trench parapets for the infantry battalions, using small English shelter segments. All night work. Nos. 1 & 3 sections employed on hutting & building a new Coy headquarters at VILLERS FAUCON	
TINCOURT	11.12.17		Nos. 1 & 3 sections relieved Nos. 2 & 4 sections	
	12.12.17 to 14.12.17		Major Dakin went to U.K. on leave. Nos. 2 & 4 Secs rested. 25 infantry were brought down to TINCOURT for relief. Divisional boundary changed & Nos. 1 & 3 sections worked making new forward billets in the Railway Cutting E of PEZIERE. 1 & 3 Secs lived at VILLERS FAUCON for the nights of 12th & 13th & moved into new forward billets on 14th.	[illegible]

A6945 Wt. W11422/M1160 350,000 12/16 D. D. & L. Forms/C./2118/14.

Major Dakin & Lieut Hewins mentioned in London Gazette of 14.12.17.

Instructions regarding War Diaries and Intelligence Summaries are contained in F. S. Regs., Part II, and the Staff Manual respectively. Title pages will be prepared in manuscript.

WAR DIARY
or
INTELLIGENCE SUMMARY.
(Erase heading not required.)

Army Form C. 2118.

Place	Date	Hour	Summary of Events and Information	Remarks and references to Appendices
TINCOURT	15.12.17		Work on shelters continued in the line	
	16.12.17		Nos. 2 & 4 Secs. relieved Nos. 1 & 3 Secs. 25 men of 6th Leics relieved 25	
			of 7th Leics. New Camp commenced between SAULCOURT & LONGAVESNES	
			as VILLERS FAUCON was out of Divisional area	
	20.12.17		No. 1 & 3 secs & 7th Leics rested	
	21.12.17		Work in line continued, also work on forward billets & new Camp	
Near SAULCOURT	24.12.17		Coy. headquarters moved to new Camp near SAULCOURT.	
	25.12.17		Nos. 2 & 4 Secs; 6th & 9th Leics. marched from PEZIERE to new Camp	
			in the morning. Men had Xmas dinners. Nos. 1 & 3 Secs. & 6th 7th & 9th	
			Leics. moved up to forward billets at night.	
	26.12.17		8th Leics. were relieved & marched from forward billets to camp & had Xmas	
			dinners. Work continued in forward & back areas.	
	28.12.17		Lt. McLaren went to U.K. on leave	
	29.12.17		Maj. Dalton returned from leave	
	31.12.17		Nos. 2 & 4 Secs. rested	

[illegible signature]

A6945 Wt. W11422/M1160 350,000 12/16 D. D. & L. Forms/C./2118/14.

CONFIDENTIAL

WAR DIARY

OF

98TH FIELD COMPANY RE

FROM 1ST JANRY 1918. TO 31ST JANRY 1918

VOLUME 28.

98TH
FIELD COMPANY,
R.E.
No. F3548.
Date 1-2-18.

Instructions regarding War Diaries and Intelligence Summaries are contained in F. S. Regs., Part II. and the Staff Manual respectively. Title pages will be prepared in manuscript.

WAR DIARY
or
~~INTELLIGENCE SUMMARY.~~
(Erase heading not required.)

Army Form C. 2118.

January 1918

Vol 29

Place	Date	Hour	Summary of Events and Information	Remarks and references to Appendices
near SAULCOURT E14b.82 Sheet 62c. 1/40000	1		No 2 & 4 Secs & one Sec attd Inf relieved No 1 & 3 Secs & 1 Sec attd Inf in forward billets in EPEHY. Work continued clearing [illegible] making [illegible] & [illegible] [illegible] work [illegible] owing to hard frost.	
	4th		No 3 Sec moved to forward billets in EPEHY	
	7th		No 1 Sec & 1 Sec attd Inf relieved No 3 Sec & one Sec attd Inf in EPEHY.	
	12th		No 3 Sec moved to forward billets near RAILTON & took over work of the 126 Fd Coy in the Left Bde Area round VAUCELLETTE FARM. 100 Inf of the 64th Bde previously attached to 126 Fd Coy attached to No 3 Sec for work.	
			Thaw set in. All work concentrated on making good and [illegible] [illegible] forward [illegible] by means of A frames & trench boards.	
	16th		3 Casualties. Work as on the 12th.	
	17		One Sec of 126 Fd Coy attached for work in the Left Bde Area	
	22		One Sec Inf relieved one Sec Inf in EPEHY.	
	29th		No 2 Sec & 1 Sec returned to HQ Camp for 4 days rest	[illegible]
	30		No 3 Sec returned to HQ Camp. Attd Inf of 64th Bde returned to 126 Fd Coy	
	31		No 3 Sec moved to forward billet in EPEHY. Work as on the 12th.	[signature illegible]

A6945 Wt. W11422/M1160 350,000 12/16 D. D. & L. Forms/C./2118/14.

1-2-18

98TH
FIELD COMPANY,
R.E.
No. 43859
Date 4-3-18.

Vol 30

CONFIDENTIAL

WAR DIARY

OF

98TH FIELD COMPANY RE

FROM 1ST FEBRUARY 1918 TO 28TH FEBRUARY 1918.

VOLUME 29.

Instructions regarding War Diaries and Intelligence Summaries are contained in F. S. Regs., Part II. and the Staff Manual respectively. Title pages will be prepared in manuscript.

WAR DIARY
or
~~INTELLIGENCE SUMMARY.~~
(*Erase heading not required.*)

February 1918

Army Form C. 2118.

Place	Date	Hour	Summary of Events and Information	Remarks and references to Appendices
SAULCOURT				
1st	1st		Nos 1, 2 & 3 Sections billeted in Epehy & 3 Section [illegible] Dug. All worked	
to	to		on revetting & reclaiming trenches that had fallen in owing to the thaw.	
7th	7th		Also putting in shelters. No 3 Section worked on the defences of [illegible]	
E14b72 Sheet 62C			EPEHY and on strengthening cellar [illegible].	
1/40000	8		All forward work taken over by 128 Fd Coy. Nos 1, 2, 3 Sections returned to H.Q.	
			Camp. SAULCOURT.	
	9		Nos 1, 2, 3, 4 Sec marched to HAUT-ALLAINES & were billeted in huts	
	10th to		All sections training in Pontoon bridging & trestle bridging all types	
	12th		of bridges being built both heavy & light.	
	13th		Inter Coy Bridging Competition each section putting one bridge over river	
			TORTILLE and two bridges of the same type	
	15		Nos 1, 2, 3 & 4 Sec returned to HQ Camp.	
	16th		Coy training, drill & musketry. No 4 Section marched to TINCOURT on 17th	
	to 28th		& started hutting for the Corps. No 2 Sec started work on a dud dugout	
			for ~~Div.~~ HQ LONGAVESNES on the 20th.	

[illegible signature] Major RE
OC 487th Fd Coy RE

A6945 Wt. W11422/M1160 350,000 12/16 D. D. & L. Forms/C./2118/14.

21st Div.

WAR
DIARY

98th FIELD COMPANY, R.E.

M A R C H

1 9 1 8

WAR DIARY

OF

98TH FIELD Co RE

FROM 1ST MARCH 1918 TO 31ST MARCH 1918

VOLUME. 30

98TH
FIELD COMPANY,
R.E.
No. 7 4042
Date 3. 4. 18.

Army Form C. 2118.

Instructions regarding War Diaries and Intelligence Summaries are contained in F. S. Regs., Part II. and the Staff Manual respectively. Title pages will be prepared in manuscript.

~~WAR DIARY or~~ INTELLIGENCE SUMMARY.

98th Field Coy R.E. (Erase heading not required.) March 1918

Vol 31

Place	Date	Hour	Summary of Events and Information	Remarks and references to Appendices
SAULCOURT	1st		No1. Sec training in H.Q. Camp. No2. Sec with attached Infantry work on Deep Dug Outs at Div Hdqtrs.	
E.14.b.7.2			LONGAVESNES. No4 Sec Hutting for Corps at TINCOURT. No3 Sec forward billet in EPEHY. Work	
Sheet 62.C.			deepened & revetting 'FIR SUPPORT' & RED LINE also providing firesteps for all round fire.	
"	4th		No4 Sec return to H.Q. Camp. Lt Allen R.E. 64 Field Coy & Lt Buchanan 7th Seaforth Highlanders (Pioneers)	
			attached for work on YELLOW & BROWN Lines with Battalions from 9th Div.	
"	5th		Digging & wiring of YELLOW LINE commenced by 64 Inf Bde under Field Coy Supervision. No 1 & 4	
			Section deepen & erect posts in the Line.	
"	6th		Digging & wiring of ~~YELLOW~~ BROWN LINE commenced by 4. S. African Infantry and one Batt. Royal Scots	
			from 9th Div under Lt Allen & Lt Buchanan.	
"	8th		No1 Sec relieves No3 Sec at EPEHY.	
"	12th		Lt Allen & Lt Buchanan return to their units. S African Infantry & Royal Scots to their Division.	
"	13th		Rifle Brigade 39th Div carry on work on BROWN LINE under Field Coy supervision.	
"	16th		No1 Sec withdrawn to H.Q. Camp & carry on work in RED LINE from there. Proceed to work in pontoons.	
"	20		No4 Sec take over work from No1 Sec in RED LINE. Work chiefly on putting gates round Posts (Inf).	
			1 Batt 39th Div work on defences GUYENCOURT.	
"	21st	4.0 a.m	Battle ~~[illegible]~~ Commenced. Billets shelled heavily for one hour & every 2 hours. 2 casualties in camp. Horses moved to the field.	

A6945 Wt. W11422/M1160 350,000 12/16 D. D. & L. Forms/C./2118/14.

Instructions regarding War Diaries and Intelligence Summaries are contained in F. S. Regs., Part II. and the Staff Manual respectively. Title pages will be prepared in manuscript.

~~WAR DIARY~~ or INTELLIGENCE SUMMARY,

(Erase heading not required.)

98th Field Coy R.E. — March 1918.

Place	Date	Hour	Summary of Events and Information	Remarks and references to Appendices
SAULCOURT	21st	7.0 am	Men stood to in Sunken Rd behind billet. Trestle equipment & two limbers	
E.14.b.7.2			damaged by shell fire. 40 other Inf join 149th Northumberland Fus as stretcher bearers.	
Sheet 62.c.		10.0 am	Transport removed from camp. Wagons sent down one at a time to fetch equipment	
			Mess & 1 pontoon hit by shells in afternoon.	
E.13.d.4.6.		5.0 pm	New camp formed with tarpaulins & tents. Patrol sent to old camp.	
"		8.0 pm	Heavy transport moved into valley near LONGAVESNES owing to Germans lengthening range.	
		5.0 pm	Company less No 2 Sec moved up to hold BROWN LINE at CAPRON COPSE & got in touch with	
			16th Div on right by means of patrols. Line was deepened where held. No casualties sustained.	
	22nd	3 am	Company relieved & return to camp. Old billet heavily shelled all day. Officer, Sergeants	
			mess, Officers mess & bicycle stand with all bicycles destroyed by shell fire.	
AIZECOURT		7 am	All transport excepting 3 pontoons & cooks cart move to AIZECOURT-LE-BAS	
-LE-BAS			Remaining wagons salve remainder of equipment from Old Billet at E.14.b.7.2 & rejoined	
D.23.b.1.7.			remainder at 4 pm at AIZECOURT-LE-BAS.	
Sheet 62.C.		12 noon	No 2 Sec withdrawn from work in Deep Dug Outs at Div Hdqrs, & the whole company & attached Infantry	
			moved into BROWN LINE in front of SAULCOURT as Infantry. Lt Shaw wounded while	
			leading No 4 Sec through barrage into SAULCOURT.	

Instructions regarding War Diaries and Intelligence Summaries are contained in F. S. Regs., Part II. and the Staff Manual respectively. Title pages will be prepared in manuscript.

INTELLIGENCE SUMMARY.

98th Field Coy R.E. (Erase heading not required.) March 1918.

Place	Date	Hour	Summary of Events and Information	Remarks and references to Appendices
AIZECOURT-LE	22nd	4 p.m.	Enemy entered SAULCOURT. Major Dakin & No 4 Sec were lost in SAULCOURT. Major Dakin last seen rallying party.	
BAS.			2/Lt Hillier, slightly wounded, & 2/Lt Wemersley retired with remainder of Company to Sunken Road South	
			of LIERAMONT.	
			Lt Hepburn killed at DRIENCOURT trying to rejoin Company from leave.	
		5 p.m.	Transport move to HAUT ALLAINES leaving under slight shell fire & machine gun fire from Aeroplanes.	
		7 p.m.	2/Lt Wemersley & remainder of Company under 62 Inf Bde take up position in GREEN LINE behind	
			AIZECOURT-LE-BAS. 2/Lt Hillier evacuated to Field ambulance.	
HAUT. ALLAINES.		9 p.m.	Transport camped at HAUT ALLAINES under 110 Inf Bde Transport Officer.	
	23rd	3 a.m.	Transport moved out of HAUT ALLAINES to FEUILLAUCOURT.	
		8 a.m.	Green line evacuated. Company completely broken up by this time. 2/Lt Wemersley remains with Inf Party.	
		8 a.m.	Transport moves West of CLERY-SUR-SOMME	
CLERY-SUR		12 mn	98th Field Coy together with 97 & 126th Field Coy combined under Major Marsden R.E. as one Field Coy.	
SOMME.		3 p.m.	Cooks, headquarters & stragglers totally 29 under 2/Lt Muirs 8 Leicestershire Regt together with	
			parties from 97th & 126th Field Coys all under Major Marsden move up to occupy a line	
			on hill in I.1.a. under Major Hewitt 8th Leic Regt, 15th D.L.I. on right. 9th K.O.Y.L.I. on left	
			Line held all night with heavy shelling later. E.A. very active in evening firing on troops.	

A6945 Wt. W11422/M1160 350,000 12/16 D. D. & L. Forms/C./2118/14.

Instructions regarding War Diaries and Intelligence Summaries are contained in F. S. Regs., Part II. and the Staff Manual respectively. Title pages will be prepared in manuscript.

~~INTELLIGENCE SUMMARY.~~

98th Field Coy RE (Erase heading not required.) March 1918

Place	Date	Hour	Summary of Events and Information	Remarks and references to Appendices
CLERY-SUR -SOMME	23rd	3 p.m	All explosives handed over to 39th Div for destruction of bridges over the SOMME.	
		3.30 p.m	Combined transport moved off to CURLU.	
CURLU	24th	9 a.m	Line at I 1.a. heavily attacked at 9.0 a.m. Orders for withdrawal received 10 a.m, enemy having penetrated the line further North.	
SUZANNE		5 a.m	Transport moved to SUZANNE arriving 8.30 a.m	
		3.30 p.m	Lt Guthrie & Lt Main with party rejoined. Remainder of 3 Coys known as 21 Div R.E. Coy	
BRAY		5.0 p.m	Moved to West of BRAY arriving at 11.0 p.m. Camped alongside road.	
L.13.c	25th	2 p.m	Moved to Wood close to CHIPILLY. Orders received 8.0 p.m to march off & dig trench	
Sheet 62.D			BRONFAY FM F 29 b. 1	
CHIPILLY		9 p.m	Party start under Lt McLaren. Orders received cancelling this work when close to BRAY	
K.34.a.28			11.40 pm [illegible] rejoins Unit.	
	26th	7 a.m	Started for RIBEMONT. Transport separated. All supplies including pontoon wagons to	
BASIEUX			No 3 Coy Train. Lts McLaren & Guthrie take parties & prepare bridges at RIBEMONT	
			& HEILLY for demolition. 1 Railway bridge & 3 road at RIBEMONT prepared. 2 Road bridges at HEILLY prepared.	
			Transport moved to D.27a. arriving 3.0 p.m. Moved again to D 31.a. & again at 10 p.m to	
			BASIEUX where it remained the night.	

Instructions regarding War Diaries and Intelligence Summaries are contained in F. S. Regs., Part II. and the Staff Manual respectively. Title pages will be prepared in manuscript.

INTELLIGENCE ~~SUMMARY.~~

98th Field Coy. R.E. (Erase heading not required.) March 1918

Place	Date	Hour	Summary of Events and Information	Remarks and references to Appendices
BASIEUX	27th	9.0 am	All sappers paraded to dig & clear out & occupy trenches D 26. Left trenches 8.0 p.m. Transport moved to BEHENCOURT.	
BEHENCOURT	28th		Lts McLaren & Guthrie returned to H.Q. having handed over Bridges to 10 Fd Engineers A.I.F.	
	29th	7.10 pm	Company moved to CARDONETTE arriving at 10.30 p.m.	
CARDONETTE	30th		Cleaning up & taking stock of deficiencies.	
	31st	10 am	Transport including surplus returned marched to HANGEST, arriving 4.15. Dismounted paraded 11.0 a.m. marched to POULAINVILLE & rode in lorries to FIXECOURT. Marched to HANGEST arriving 6.35 p.m.	
			Casualties 21–31st: 1 Officer Killed	
			2 " 19 O.R. Wounded	
			1 " 23 O.R. Missing	
			W. A. J. McLaren Lt. R.E. for O.C. 98th Fd. Co. R.E.	

A6945 Wt. W11422/M1160 350,000 12/16 D. D. & L. Forms/C./2118/14.

21st Divisional Engineers

98th FIELD COMPANY R.E. ::: APRIL 1918.

98TH
FIELD COMPANY,
R.E.
No. 2/4255
Date 30-4-18

Vol 32

CONFIDENTIAL

WAR DIARY

OF

98TH FIELD COMPANY R.E.

FROM 1ST APRIL 1918. TO 30TH APRIL 1918.

VOLUME 31.

Instructions regarding War Diaries and Intelligence Summaries are contained in F. S. Regs., Part II. and the Staff Manual respectively. Title pages will be prepared in manuscript.

WAR DIARY

or

~~INTELLIGENCE SUMMARY.~~

(Erase heading not required.)

Army Form C. 2118.

Place	Date	Hour	Summary of Events and Information	Remarks and references to Appendices
PESELHOEK	2/4/18		Company detrained Peselhoek and proceeded to LOCRE.	
LOCRE	3/4/18		Capt. A. H. SOUTAR joined Coy from 124 Field Coy RE to take Command.	
	4/4/18		Coy moved by march to R.E. Farm. Sheet 28.	
	5/4/18		Takes over line in Wytschaete area.	
	6/4/18		Work on gas proofing dugouts etc.	
	7/4/18		Coy Relieved by 82nd Field Coy RE.	
	10/4/18		Move to Vauban Camp H 30. Sheet 28. & Take over work from 458 Field Coy RE.	
	11th – 14th		Work on Dumbarton Switch and gas proofing dugouts.	
	15th		Coy digs strong points in ~~[illegible]~~ Trench farm – Lock 8 – Voormezeele line.	
	16th		Move to Winnipeg camp work on GHQ 2nd line	
	17th		Lts. RAY. R.M. BOYD-MOSS H.L.I., CADELL R.E. BOOTES G. joined from Base.	
	17th – 25th		Work on GHQ 2nd line from RIDGE WOOD to SWAN CHA.	
	20th		Lt. G. BOOTES posted to 97th Field Coy R.E. & left to take up duties	
	24th		Work on Switch line DICKEBUSCH LAKE to GHQ1 at English Wood	
	25th		Same work	
	26th – 30th		Work on G.H.Q 2nd line at ANZAC CAMP H.30 Sheet 28	

A H Soutar Capt RE
OC 95 Field Coy RE

A6945 Wt. W11422/M1160 350,000 12/16 D. D. & L. Forms/C./2118/14.

CONFIDENTIAL

WAR DIARY

OF

98TH FIELD COMPANY R.E.

FROM 1ST MAY 1918 TO 31ST MAY 1918

VOLUME No 32

98TH
FIELD COMPANY
R.E.
No. F4473
Date 6-6-18

Instructions regarding War Diaries and Intelligence Summaries are contained in F. S. Regs., Part II. and the Staff Manual respectively. Title pages will be prepared in manuscript.

WAR DIARY
or
~~INTELLIGENCE SUMMARY~~
(Erase heading not required.)

Army Form C. 2118.

Vol 33

Place	Date	Hour	Summary of Events and Information	Remarks and references to Appendices
Near BUSSEBOOM	1/5/18		Company relieved by 82nd Field Coy RE.	
STEENVOORDE	2/5/18		Company move by march route to BOIS DE STEENVOORDE and bivouac for the night	
BUYSSCHEURE	3/5/18		Company move by route march to BUYSSCHEURE	
	4/5/18		Company marches to WIZERNES and entrains 23-15. Men 40 per truck & very crowded.	
ANTHENAY	6/5/18		Company detrains at SAVIGNY sur Ardre and marches to billets at ANTHENAY.	
"	7/5/18		Coy in billets, rest & clean up.	
"	8/5/18		Training. Attached infantry return to their units	
LHERY	12/5/18		Coy. moved to LHERY into billets	
PROUILLY	13/5/18		Coy moved to Camp near PROUILLY	
HERMONVILLE	14/5/18		Coy. moved to HERMONVILLE into billets and took over work from	
"			13/14 Compagnie du Génie	
			Worked on construction of dugouts for M.G. Battalion, screening of roads	
"	to		construction of trench monorail, making of firesteps, gas proofing	
			of dugouts. Attached infantry returned on 17/5/18. Wagons remained	
"	20/5/18		in HERMONVILLE, and horses & drivers at LES GRATIERES.	
	21/5/18		Lt. McLaren went on leave to PARIS.	

A6945 Wt. W11422/M1160 350,000 12/16 D. D. & L. Forms/C./2118/14.

Instructions regarding War Diaries and Intelligence Summaries are contained in F. S. Regs., Part II. and the Staff Manual respectively. Title pages will be prepared in manuscript.

WAR DIARY
or
~~INTELLIGENCE~~ SUMMARY.
(*Erase heading not required.*)

Army Form C. 2118.

Place	Date	Hour	Summary of Events and Information	Remarks and references to Appendices
HERMONVILLE	24/5/18		Capt. Gregson proceeded to ETAPLES on duty. Lt. Mitchell rejoined	
			Work continued.	
"	26/5/18		Lt. Womersley M.C. and 12 NCO's & men took part in a raid on the enemy trenches. Two Bangalore torpedoes were successfully exploded, destroying the wire. No casualties.	
"			2/Lt. Kay proceeded to Gas School at LHERY	
	27/5/18		Dismounted portion of Coy. & attached infantry manned battle positions N.W. of HERMONVILLE at 12.45 am. under heavy gas & H.E. shelling. Transport moved out of HERMONVILLE to a wood S. of LUTHERNAY FARM on the PÉVY road. Coy. H.Q. moved to CHATEAU DE ST. REMY. Lt. Womersley MC and 2/Lt. Boyd Moss were wounded about 4am. & 7 O.R. killed and 4 wounded. At 6 pm. the Coy. was relieved in its battle position by the French & took up another line at	
"			64 Inf. Bde. H.Q. at CHAMPIGNONNIERES.	
BRANSCOURT	28/5/18		Transport moved at 3 am to BRANSCOURT. After bombardment, Coy. was attacked in flank at 8.30 am. Bombardment lasted 4 hours and Trench Mortars were used by the Germans in addition to guns. The Coy. was forced to withdraw without officers, leaving Major Soutar M.C. and	

Army Form C. 2118.

Instructions regarding War Diaries and Intelligence Summaries are contained in F. S. Regs., Part II. and the Staff Manual respectively. Title pages will be prepared in manuscript.

WAR DIARY
or
INTELLIGENCE SUMMARY.
(Erase heading not required.)

Place	Date	Hour	Summary of Events and Information	Remarks and references to Appendices
BRANSCOURT	28/5/18		2/Lt CADELL wounded. 2/Lt. MOSS, the attached infantry officer was killed. The remainder of No. 2 Sec. was retained in support to the	
to	to		French near TRIGNY till the morning of 29/5/18 after which they rejoined	
VILLE EN TARDENOIS	29/5/18		the Coy. Nos. 1, 3, & 4 Secs. rejoined the transport at VILLE EN TARDENOIS on 28/5/18. Transport had moved at 10.30 am. on 28/5/18 to VILLE EN TARDENOIS.	
MARFAUX	29/5/18		Transport moved with Coy. to MARFAUX.	
FORÊT D'EPERNAY	30/5/18		Coy. moved to FORÊT D'EPERNAY. All bridging equipment was dumped on the way at DAMÈRY to form a bridge over the R. MARNE.	
ÊTRECHY	31/5/18		Coy. moved to bivouac in a wood about 1 mile S.E. of ÊTRECHY. It was unofficially reported that 2/Lt. KAY had been admitted to C.C.S. at EPERNAY. sick.	

Casualties for the month

	Officers	O.R.	Attd. Officers	Attd. O.R.
Killed	–	9	1	1
Wounded	2	19		2
Wounded & Missing	2	-		–
Missing		28		58

[illegible] Capt RE
a/O.C. [illegible] Coy RE
2/6/18

A6945 Wt. W11422/M1160 350,000 12/16 D. D. & L. Forms/C./2118/14.

CONFIDENTIAL

WAR DIARY

OF

98TH FIELD COMPANY R.E.

FROM 1st JUNE 1918 TO 30TH JUNE 1918

VOLUME 23

Army Form C. 2118.

Instructions regarding War Diaries and Intelligence Summaries are contained in F. S. Regs., Part II, and the Staff Manual respectively. Title pages will be prepared in manuscript.

WAR DIARY
or
~~INTELLIGENCE SUMMARY.~~
(*Erase heading not required.*)

JUNE 1918.

Place	Date	Hour	Summary of Events and Information	Remarks and references to Appendices
				8R 34
ETRECHY (Chalons, 50 / 80,000)	1		Company resting. Capt. Ferguson, R.E., returned.	
	2		Company resting	
	3		Coy moved with 110th I.B. Group to Courgeonnet: bivouaced in open outside village	
			Lt. (A/Capt.) W.L. CAMPBELL, R.E., from 126 Fd Coy R.E., took command of Company.	
Courgeonnet. (Chalons, 50 / 80,000).	4th–8th		Coy resting & training: drill, musketry, demolitions & schemes for N.C.O.s. Total strength of Nos 1, 2, 3 & 4 sections – 60.	
	9th		Lt. McLaren, R.E., with C.S.M. & 40 O.R. proceeded by lorry to join Composite Fd Coy R.E. (under Maj. Marsden, R.E., 126 Coy, R.E.) with 21st Independent Brigade, at Igny. Coy moved at 11 a.m. with 110th I.B. to billets at Verdey.	
Verdey (Arcis, 67 / 80,000)	10th–12th		Coy resting & cleaning up. Warning order for move by train to Abbeville Area any day after 12th.	
	13th		Coy moved at noon with 110th I.B. Group, via Sezanne, Connantre, Fere Champenoise to	
CONNANTRAY (Arcis, 67 / 80,000)			CONNANTRAY, the staging area. About 20 miles: arrived 8.30 p.m.	
	14th		Moved at 3 p.m. to entraining station, SOMMESOUS. Waited there from 5 p.m. to 9 p.m. till train came in; sharing it with 7th Leicester Regt. Plenty room for men & horses, but had to leave 1 G.S. waggon to come on next train. Entrained by 10.30 p.m., & left at 11 p.m.	
	15th		Train all day, via Romilly-sur-Seine, St. Denis, Pontoise, Serqueux & Amiens (outskirts).	

A6945 Wt. W11422/M1160 350,000 12/16 D. D. & L. Forms/C./2118/14.

Instructions regarding War Diaries and Intelligence Summaries are contained in F. S. Regs., Part II. and the Staff Manual respectively. Title pages will be prepared in manuscript.

WAR DIARY
or
~~INTELLIGENCE SUMMARY.~~
(Erase heading not required.)

Army Form C. 2118.

JUNE, 1918.

Place	Date	Hour	Summary of Events and Information	Remarks and references to Appendices
	16th		Reached Hangest-sur-Somme at 10 a.m.: detrained by 3 a.m., & moved off under	Amiens 1/100,000
Buzménard			110th Bde orders at 4 a.m. Marched via Airaines, Oisemont to Buzménard (20 miles) &	
(Dieppe 1/100,000)			arrived 12 noon. Village very small, & billets not good.	
	17th		Rest day.	
	18th		Capt Gregson R.E. to C.R.E.s to act as Adjutant. 2Lts D. M. Menzies & L. W. Lillingston R.E.	
			reported for duty from R.E.B.D.	
	19th		Lt. Maclaren R.E. & party from Composite [illegible] Coy rejoined company: been employed	
			on making "points d'appui" in a wood S.E. of Try, & in Bois de Crochet, S. of Trossy: also on defences	
			of Cesent. (Chalons 50/[illegible] 20,000 sheet.) Besides other 2 O.R. wounded by shelling of billets.	
	20th		Rest day.	
	21st		Bathing parade, & clean up of waggons. Warning order for move to Monchy-sur-Eu area tomorrow.	
	22nd		Moved with 110th I.B. Group at 10 a.m., via Bouttencourt, Martières, Sorcng, Bazinval, Melleville to	
Etocquigny			Etocquigny, about 20 miles. Accomodation very bad: most of coy. in bivouacs	
	23rd		O.C. reconnoitring site for rifle range for 110th I.B., to fire up to 400 yds. Coy resting.	
	24th		Small party marked out range, which is immediately S. of Bois de Gaumont, on Sept Meules-Londinières road	
Baromesnil.			Coy moved at 3 p.m. to better billets in Baromesnil; water for horses to be carted from R. Yeres.	
			O.s C. conference at 37th Hdqrs Gamaches, on Training. Order from Bde to stop work on range.	

Instructions regarding War Diaries and Intelligence Summaries are contained in F. S. Regs., Part II. and the Staff Manual respectively. Title pages will be prepared in manuscript.

WAR DIARY
or
~~INTELLIGENCE SUMMARY.~~
(*Erase heading not required.*)

Army Form C. 2118.

JUNE 1918.

Place	Date	Hour	Summary of Events and Information	Remarks and references to Appendices
Dieppe 1/100,000				
Boromesnil	25th		C.R.E. called in morning with information that Div. moving about 28th to St. Omer Area.	
			II Lt. E.F. Molony R.E. reported for duty from 126 Fd Coy R.E.	
	26th		Sections training in morning. Orders from Bde that move is cancelled temporarily & to start work on new range tomorrow. Orders from C.R.E. to get out training programme on basis of one month to be spent in this area.	
	27th		Nos 1 & 2 sections started work on new range with 120 working party from 6th Leics. Gallery 8' deep to be dug for 16 targets 6'x6', & two firing points to be made (100x & 200x ranges). Nos 3 & 4 sections on billet improvement & making 30x range for company use	
	28th		Work as yesterday. Epidemic of influenza breaking out in company - mild so far.	
	29th		Work as usual: working party on range provided by 1st Wilts Regt, who have taken place of 8th Leics Regt in 110th I.B. Range 75% complete.	
			Warning order that Div. moving very soon: transport probably tomorrow & dismounted personnel on July 1st.	
	30th		Coy transport moved off 9.30am to join 110th I.B. Transport Group & proceed to OISEMONT.	
			Dismounted personnel moving tomorrow by train to Pucheviller's Area.	

M. Campbell Major R.E.
O.C. 98 Fd. Coy R.E.

A6945 Wt. W11422/M1160 350,000 12/16 D. D. & L. Forms/C./2118/14.

CONFIDENTIAL

WAR DIARY.

OF

98th FIELD COY R.E.

FROM 1st JULY 1918. TO 31st JULY 1918.

VOLUME 34.

98TH
FIELD COMPANY,
R.E.
No. F4994
Date 31-7-18

Instructions regarding War Diaries and Intelligence Summaries are contained in F. S. Regs., Part II. and the Staff Manual respectively. Title pages will be prepared in manuscript.

WAR DIARY
or
~~INTELLIGENCE SUMMARY.~~
(Erase heading not required.)

98th Field Coy RE — Army Form C. 2118.

JULY, 1918.

Vol 35

Place	Date	Hour	Summary of Events and Information	Remarks and references to Appendices
	1st		Dismounted portion of Coy. left Bovencourt 3am arrived Eu station 5am. Loaded that portion of Coy transport being conveyed by rail. Train left 9.30am, via Abbeville to	
Sheet 57D 1/40,000			Candas: arrived 3.30pm. Detrained, offloaded wagons & marched to billets in Beauquesne, arriving 9pm. Billets fair.	
Beauquesne	2nd		Rest day & cleaning up	
	3rd		Transport rejoined 8am. Owing to influenza, only 30 sappers available for work.	
	4th		71 O.R. reported as reinforcements from base: majority just out from England	
	5th		Officers of coy on reconnaissance to Acheux Wood to see positions taken up in case of Alarm. The coy attached to 110th I.B. who assemble in Brown Line in Forceville - Beaussart sector. Trenches 3' deep in most places, but badly blown around Beaussart.	
	6th		Coy. training in morning: drill, musketry, P.T., & games in afternoon. Weather fine.	
	7th		Church Parade with 97th & 126th Fd. Coys RE at 9.30am. Officers & senior N.C.O.s to No 7 RE Park Rosel, to see Moir M.G. Pillbox in course of erection	
	8th		1 N.C.O. & 6 sappers with 25 men from 14th N.F.(P) working on Adv. Div. H.Q. - O.17.b.6.9	
			Lt. McLaren, R.E. on 10 days French leave, from 10th - 19th: also C.S.M. & 1 O.R.	
			Coy. training & preparing for Corps Commander's inspection. Capt Gregson RE returned to duty from C.R.E. 21 Div.	

A6945 Wt. W11422/M1160 350,000 12/16 D. D. & L. Forms/C./2118/14.

Instructions regarding War Diaries and Intelligence Summaries are contained in F. S. Regs., Part II. and the Staff Manual respectively. Title pages will be prepared in manuscript.

WAR DIARY
or
~~INTELLIGENCE SUMMARY.~~
(Erase heading not required.)

Army Form C. 2118.

JULY 1918

Place	Date	Hour	Summary of Events and Information	Remarks and references to Appendices
Beauquesne	9th		Nos 1 & 2 sections training. Nos 3 & 4 sections under Lts. Molony & Lillingston left at 5 p.m. to proceed to billets in Acheux for work on Brown Line, under CE V Corps instructions.	
	10th		97, 96 & 126th Fd Coys RE, with 62nd I.B. inspected near Beauquesne by V Corps Commander. Transport paraded independently & inspected after dismounted parade. Corps Commander not pleased with condition of horses, harness or wagons. 3 & 4 sections working on Brown Line system from P28a 5.0 to P22c 7.5, 9/14th Bn N.F. (P) working north of this. Trench in this sector quite fightable, so main work on clearing crops to give field of fire & strengthening wire.	
	11th		No 2 section working on completion of baths at Puchevillers. No 1 sec. on repainting all wagons. V Corps Horsemaster inspected all horses, & reported them as being clean & well looked after.	
	12th		Work as before. Weather showery.	
	13th		Work as before.	
	14th		Rest day. O.C. No 124th Fd Coy RE (38th Div) billeted at P26 central, to arrange for relief about 18th inst. 12 men (3 per section) attached to 1st Bn. Mid'x Regt. for instruction in L.G. work, in view of the fact that 4 Lewis Guns are to be issued to Fd Coys, in addition to the one for A.A. work.	

Instructions regarding War Diaries and Intelligence Summaries are contained in F. S. Regs., Part II. and the Staff Manual respectively. Title pages will be prepared in manuscript.

WAR DIARY
or
~~INTELLIGENCE SUMMARY.~~
(Erase heading not required.)

Army Form C. 2118.

July 1918

Place	Date	Hour	Summary of Events and Information	Remarks and references to Appendices
Sheet 57D				
Beauquesne	15th		Officers of Coy. round centre sector V Corps front, taking over work in hand from 124th Fd Coy RE	
	16th		Nos 1&2 secs. training. Orders for relief of 38th Div on 16th inst in Englebelmer sector. These were cancelled at night owing to reorganisation of Corps front. Heavy thunderstorms.	
	17th		Nos 1&2 secs training; 3&4 secs work on Brown Line. Capt Greyson, RE proceeded on duty to England to join R.A.F.	
	18th		As yesterday.	
	19th		Lt. Col. Addison, CMG, DSO, RE called in morning to say goodbye to Coy on parade. Lt. Col. Masters DSO RE CRE 21 Div. visited coy. Nos 3&4 secs relieved in Acheux by one section 97 Coy RE & returned to Coy. Hdqrs. Lt McLaren RE returned from French leave. Lt. W.T. Vaughan-Williams, MC, RE joined for duty from R.E.B.D. Lt McLaren appointed 2nd in command of Coy & to be a/Captain from 19th inst.	
	20th		Company training. Weather very unsettled.	
	21st		Rest day: Church Parade & Coy. sports in afternoon. Lt. H.E. Harben, RE reported for duty from 1st Siege Coy, R.A. R.E.	
	22nd		Coy training. O.C. Conference at CREs on work to be done in line (Mailly Sector). Orders for relief of 63rd Div. on 25th inst. in Mailly Sector.	
	23rd		O.C. to billets of 247 Fd Coy RE, 63rd (R.N.) Div., taking over work & round line. Heavy rain. Lt. Harben on leave to U.K.	
	24th		Sec officers round line with opposite numbers of 247 Fd Coy, RE.	
Englebelmer	25th		Sections moved off independently about 9 a.m. No 2 to Englebelmer, Nos 1&4 to P10 d 2.2 & Coy. Hdqrs & No 3 to P24 c 2.2. Transport lines [illegible] Relief completed by 10.30 a.m.	

A6945 Wt. W11422/M1160 350,000 12/16 D. D. & L. Forms/C./2118/14.

Army Form C. 2118.

Instructions regarding War Diaries and Intelligence Summaries are contained in F. S. Regs., Part II. and the Staff Manual respectively. Title pages will be prepared in manuscript.

WAR DIARY

or

~~INTELLIGENCE SUMMARY.~~

(Erase heading not required.)

JULY, 1918

Place	Date	Hour	Summary of Events and Information	Remarks and references to Appendices
Sheet 57 D. Englebelmer	26th		No 2 section attached to Bde for work in Forward Zone. Rest of Coy under C.R.E.'s orders. No 3 section working on Intermediate system, & C dugout at Q20b.6.2. No 4 section on Purple system, & supervising R.F.A. dugouts near Englebelmer, & erection of 3 Moir Pill Boxes. Coy working in Right Bde sector, with 110th Inf Bde. Boundaries: Drake Alley, Cross Avenue to Q27b.0.4, thence W. along Grid line, & Quaker Alley to Q16d.0.6, thence W. along Grid line.	
	27th		Work started night 26/27th. Working Parties: No 2 sec. 40 men from both Right & Left Bns. for work on Baro Trench & Ridge Trench: No 3 sec. - 1 coy from both Right & Left Bns for work on Intermediate Line of Resistance, just E of Hill 142: No 4 sec. - 1 coy from Reserve Bn for work on Purple System.	
	28th		Trenches very bad after rain - all require draining, & sides sloping properly.	
	29th		Work as usual. Heavy gas shelling on division area during night 28/29th & 29/30th. 3 men on Special leave to U.K., & 2 on Paris leave.	
	30th		O.C. with C.R.E. round Purple System. Sites of posts decided on. Work as usual.	
	31st		Handed over work on Moir Pill Boxes to 97 Fd Coy R.E. & took over from them work on dugout Q3d9.5, & supervision of R.F.A. Dug Out N. of Mailly (No 4 section). Other work as usual.	

[illegible] Major R.E.
O.C. [illegible] Fd Coy R.E.

A6945 Wt. W11422/M1160 350,000 12/16 D. D. & L. Forms/C./2118/14.

CONFIDENTIAL

WAR DIARY.

OF

98TH FIELD COY. RE

FROM 1ST AUGUST 1918. TO 31ST AUGUST 1918

VOLUME 35

98TH
FIELD COMPANY,
R.E.
No. 75296
Dated 31-8-18

Instructions regarding War Diaries and Intelligence Summaries are contained in F. S. Regs., Part II. and the Staff Manual respectively. Title pages will be prepared in manuscript.

WAR DIARY
or
~~INTELLIGENCE SUMMARY.~~
(Erase heading not required.)

Army Form C. 2118.

Vol 36

AUGUST, 1918.

Place	Date	Hour	Summary of Events and Information	Remarks and references to Appendices
Sheet 57D.S.E. 1/20,000				
Englebelmer P24c.2.2.	1		No 2 Section working on posts in Forward Zone, with total working party of from 4 to 6 platoons	
			No 3 Section working on Intermediate Zone (H.11.142) total working party 6–8 platoons	
			No 4 Section working on Purple — — (Englebelmer Line) total working party of 4 platoons	
			No 1 Section on dug outs & odd jobs. Trench work mostly drainage & revetment of fire steps	
			Trenchboards extremely scarce, but supply of revetting material improving.	
	2		Work as usual.	
	3.		Enemy withdrawal to E of Ancre. Weather very wet.	
	4–8		Work as usual. Weather clearing, & good progress being made on trenches. Total	
			allotment of trenchboards for Bde sector, since coming into the line is about 300.	
	9		110th Inf Bde extending line about 500 yds North. Boundary now Etonbeare, Trigger Av. to Q14c0.0.	
			Lt Harbord R.E. returned from leave: Capt McLaren R.E. on leave to U.K.	
	10		Started work on Etor Lane, which is in very bad state, but this work taken over by Pioneers.	
			Signs of enemy withdrawal opposite Army front. No 1 Section moved to Coy H.Qrs from P10d2.2.	
	11–13		Work as usual. 130 War Savings Certifs. bought within last week by 60 men. Weather fine	
	14		Work as usual during day. Orders from C.R.E. at 7 p.m placing coy under 110th Inf Bde for	
			making crossings over Ancre. Infantry patrols pushed across river, but driven back.	
			3 Sections, moved to Forward Area in position of readiness, but nothing done.	

A6945 Wt. W11422/M1160 350,000 12/16 D. D. & L. Forms/C./2118/14.

Army Form C. 2118.

WAR DIARY
or
INTELLIGENCE SUMMARY.
(Erase heading not required.)

Instructions regarding War Diaries and Intelligence Summaries are contained in F. S. Regs., Part II. and the Staff Manual respectively. Title pages will be prepared in manuscript.

AUGUST, 1918.

Place	Date	Hour	Summary of Events and Information	Remarks and references to Appendices
Sheet 57c S.E. 1/20,000 Englebelmer (P24c 2.2)				
	15.		Nos 1 & 2 secs under Lt. Menzies relieved Nos 3 & 4 secs in Forward Zone at 6 p.m. Ordered out at 8 p.m. to work on Mill Crossing Q24c 4.2, but infantry patrols again pushed back W. of River & nothing done. Good reconnaissance by Lt. Menzies of Mill Crossing & River Area in Q24c.	
	16.		Normal work being resumed shortly but forward sections remaining up in readiness.	
	17		Orders from 110th Inf. Bde. to make good two crossings for infantry in file tonight, but these orders cancelled by a Div. Order stating no patrols to be done east of River. Nos 1 & 2 secs worked on Forward Zone & returned to Coy. Hdqrs. at 10 p.m. 3 & 4 secs working as usual but without infantry parties.	
	18.		Nos 1 & 2 sections rest day: 3 & 4 secs work as usual on Inter. & Purple Systems.	
	19.		Work as usual.	
	20.		Work till midday, then sections returned to camp. 110th Bde side slipping North tonight: boundaries Quaker Alley & E & W. Grid Line through Q18c 0.0. Conference at 126 Coy HQ in afternoon with CRE with regard to crossings over R. Ancre for infantry in file. 2 sections placed at disposal of 110th Bde for this purpose. Nos 3 & 4 secs under Lts Molony & Lillings to(?) moved at 10 p.m. to a position of readiness at Q11b 0.4, where dump of light bridging material was made by OC. Sections caught in heavy gas shelling in Ravine(?), Inf. & Beaumont & Hamel valley gassed during night.	

A6945 Wt. W11422/M1160 350,000 12/16 D. D. & L. Forms/C./2118/14.

Instructions regarding War Diaries and Intelligence Summaries are contained in F. S. Regs., Part II. and the Staff Manual respectively. Title pages will be prepared in manuscript.

Army Form C. 2118.

WAR DIARY
or
~~INTELLIGENCE SUMMARY.~~
(Erase heading not required.)

AUGUST, 1918.

Place	Date	Hour	Summary of Events and Information	Remarks and references to Appendices
Sheet 57D S.E. 1/20,000.				
	21		Lt Molony slightly wounded whilst carrying stores to river with sections.	
		12 noon	Lt Wellington(?) & Molony with 69 men of 3rd & 4th sections to F.A., suffering from gas effects.	
		2 pm	Lt Menzies with 1 & 2 sections moved up to position of readiness. 110th Bde had not obtained	
	22	2 am	footing on E bank of river; 1 & 2 sections made good two crossings for infantry with covering party in front, then returned to forward position Bovet Trench Q9c.	
			1 & 2 sections out at night endeavouring to make a third crossing, but no work possible owing to gas shelling. 110th Bde relieved by 50th Bde. 2 sections returned to	
	23	6 am	camp P24c2.2. 5 pm Orders from CRE to put Weldon Trestle Bridge over Ancre at P9a9.6 after attack tomorrow. Nos 1 & 2 sections, & 2 sections 126 Coy RE allotted for this purpose. Coy moved 6 pm to P12 central, & there joined by transport.	
	24	2 am	Orders from CRE to proceed to make bridge. Moved off 3 am & picked up 3 Trestle wagons & 2 sections 126 Coy at Fluchevillers(?). Unloaded wagons at	
		7 am	R3c5.1 at 7 am, but then shelled with gas & H.E. Bridge under direct enemy view from R11b, so withdrew sections temporarily. Recommenced work	
		12 noon	at midday, & bridge completed (2 Trestles in span of 45'), with approaches from main roads on either side by about 3 pm.	
			No enemy interference during erection. First 4 ton bridge about 3.30 pm	

Instructions regarding War Diaries and Intelligence Summaries are contained in F. S. Regs., Part II. and the Staff Manual respectively. Title pages will be prepared in manuscript.

WAR DIARY

or

~~INTELLIGENCE SUMMARY.~~

(*Erase heading not required.*)

Army Form C. 2118.

AUGUST, 1918.

Place	Date	Hour	Summary of Events and Information	Remarks and references to Appendices
Sheet 57D S.E. 1/20,000				
	25		Parade 9am for work on converting Heinzmann's Path into track for pack transport. Helping 1/2 Coy on this job & work till 6pm. 2 pontoon wagons on carting stores for this work. Coy moved to Puchevillers about [illegible] 8.6. Capt McLaren returned from leave to U.K.	
	26.		Parade 3am for work on water supply for horses at Miraumont, R50.5.5. 60 ft. troughing erected, together with approaches etc. made from German [illegible] frames. Coy moved to Battery Valley, about R8d, with 97 & 120 [illegible]	
	27.		Coy employed on augmenting water supply at Miraumont. Weather becoming unsettled.	
	28.		No sections erecting horse troughs at P15, & completing Miraumont horse water point. 120 ft. troughing erected together with standings & approaches. No 2 section commenced water point at R8b14, also [illegible] 12 mines dug out from Miraumont - P15 Road. 2Lt. A.H. St. Johnston, R.E. reported for duty from R.E.B.D.	
	29.		P15 water point completed, also 50 ft. troughing at R8b14, & 36 ft troughing at R4c5.8, with approaches in both cases. No 3 sec commenced new horse water point at R4d5.1.	
Sheet 57C S.W. 1/20,000	30.		Coy moved to M16d.50.95. No 1 & 2 secs completing water point at R4d5.1: 50 ft. troughing erected, & 100 yards approach & standings planked.	
	31.		Coy employed on repair of Ligny-Thilloy-Factory Corner Road, N19c9.1.	

[Signature], [illegible]

[illegible] 98

A6945 Wt. W11422/M1160 350,000 12/16 D. D. & L. Forms/C./2118/14.

VR 37

Confidential

War Diary

of

98th Field Coy R.E.

From 1st Sept 1918 To 30th Sept 1918.

Volume 36.

Instructions regarding War Diaries and Intelligence Summaries are contained in F. S. Regs., Part II. and the Staff Manual respectively. Title pages will be prepared in manuscript.

WAR DIARY

~~or~~

~~INTELLIGENCE SUMMARY.~~

(*Erase heading not required.*)

Army Form C. 2118.

SEPTEMBER 1918

Place	Date	Hour	Summary of Events and Information	Remarks and references to Appendices
Sheet 57c S.W. 1/20,000.				
Butte de Warlencourt			Coy. strength 5 officers 166 O.R. (practically 2 sections deficient)	
	1.		Coy employed on repair of Le Sars – Eaucourt Road & Factory Corner – Ligny Thilloy Road till midday when recalled by C.R.E.'s orders. Orders to make 2 strong pts in vicinity of Beaulencourt (captured by	
			110th I. Bde this morning) to guard against counter attacks from N.E. & S.E. 2 sections 126 Coy R.E.	
	2		allotted in addition to 96 Coy R.E. for this purpose. Pts completed by 1.30 am. 1 O.R. (126 Coy) wounded.	
			Secs returned to camp 4 am & in camp all day. Advance continues & Villers-au-Flos captured.	
	3.		Work as on 1/9/18, with 2 platoons 14 N.F. (P) in addition working on relief track for horses	
			round N.W. edge of Le Sars – completed. Well reconnaissance of Beaulencourt, but none found.	
	4.		Observed as day of rest.	
	5		Coy standing by to move forward. Orders for relief of 151 Fd Coy R.E. (38th Div). ~~Found~~ them	
			assisting 123 Fd Coy R.E. (38th Div) on putting a light & a medium pontoon bridge over Canal du Nord	
Sheet 57c 1/40,000			at V.8.c.8.6. 2 sections 97 Fd Coy R.E. allotted in addition to 96 Coy R.E. for all bridging	
			work over canal. Company (less transport) moved to T.17.b. in afternoon. 2 secs 97 Fd Coy	
	6		relieved 38th Div Coys on bridges 3 am. Found both pontoon bridges across (120' width of water)	
			but approaches on both banks very bad, involving ramps of 1 in 2 places. 2 secs 96 Fd Coy R.E.	
			relieved 97 Coy R.E. 7 am. Work concentrated on ramps. Orders from C.R.E. at night	
			that medium bridge not to be made fit for transport, only infantry in fours.	

A6945 Wt. W11422/M1160 350,000 12/16 D. D. & L. Forms/C./2118/14.

Instructions regarding War Diaries and Intelligence Summaries are contained in F. S. Regs., Part II. and the Staff Manual respectively. Title pages will be prepared in manuscript.

WAR DIARY
or
~~INTELLIGENCE SUMMARY.~~
(*Erase heading not required.*)

Army Form C. 2118.

SEPTEMBER, 1918.

Place	Date	Hour	Summary of Events and Information	Remarks and references to Appendices
Sheet 57C 1/40,000.				
Marancourt	7.		Coy moved off 7 a.m. to new camp in U18c, & were joined by transport. Secs working on pontoon bridges, making infantry crossings over demolished steel bridge at V8c5.0, & a floating duckboard crossing at V14a.3.8. 2 secs. 97 Coy RE joined on this work from 2pm	
	8		Work on bridges as yesterday. Crossing at V8c5.0 completed. Reconnaissance of hut accomodation in Div. Area	
	9		Assisting 126 Coy RE on horse water points along canal, & started conversion of German concrete block factory into Div. Baths. 6 spray Baths working under Sapper Arm... 30 reinforcements reported. Weather showery.	
	10.		Work on repair of cross country track from U15a.6.2 to U11b.5.1. Div. Baths at V8c9.8, & repair of 2 wells at Fins Crossroads V12c7.6. Orders for 3 secs to be attached to 110th Inf Bde [illegible] remainder of coy. to continue work as usual, & to take over horse water points from 126 Fd Coy RE.	
	11.		No 2 sec. working on baths, horse troughs along canal, & notice boarding Div. Area E. of canal. Nos 1&3 secs. moved off 2pm to billets at V18c2.9. (110th Bde H.Q.). Weather unsettled	
	12		No 2 sec. work as before. Nos 1&3 secs. working for Bde.	
	13.		Work as before. Reconnaissance for cross country tracks from Nurlu–Fins road to forward area. Two Bde groups of tracks, with 3 tracks per group, each track for infantry in fours. Northern group from W18a, north of Sorel-le-Grand & Heudecourt to Railton, W16d. Southern group from V23b, south of villages to W23c.	

Instructions regarding War Diaries and Intelligence Summaries are contained in F. S. Regs., Part II. and the Staff Manual respectively. Title pages will be prepared in manuscript.

WAR DIARY ~~or~~ ~~INTELLIGENCE SUMMARY.~~

(Erase heading not required.)

Army Form C. 2118.

SEPTEMBER 1918

Place	Date	Hour	Summary of Events and Information	Remarks and references to Appendices
Sheet 57c		1/40,000		
Manancourt	13		2Lt. W.H. Cullis R.E. reported for duty from R.E.B.D. 3 O.R. wounded (Bde section)	
	14		No 2 sec. with 1 Coy Pioneers (16th N.F.) working on cross country tracks. One track per group completed. Tracks marked by pickets every 30 yards connected by wire with tracing tape.	
	15		Work on tracks as before. Nos 1 & 3 secs returned to Coy. Billets on relief of Bde, having worked for 4 nights on making posts in & deepening front line in W24 a & b d.	
	16		Nos 2 & 3 secs with 1 Coy Pioneers on tracks. No 4 section on repairs of dugouts & shelters at Brickyard, W21c44, for use as Bde H.Q. Tracks practically complete.	
	17		Northern group of tracks alignment altered for about 2 miles owing to a change in Div. Boundary. Whole Coy & 1½ Coys Pioneers employed on this. Tracks completed. Conference at C.R.E.s on consolidation work after coming attack.	
	18		Major Campbell goes on French leave. O.C. 97th Field Coy R.E., Major Poole N.F. (Pioneers) & Capt McLaren reconnoitre positions for Strong Points. 4 Strong Points dug during the night on a line through X.14.c & X.20.c. 4 O.R. casualties.	
	19		Work on Strong Points taken over by 11th Field Coy. R.E. Lt Stockdale T.F. R.E. & 2 O.R. reported for duty	

A6945 Wt. W11422/M1160 350,000 12/16 D. D. & L. Forms/C./2118/14.

Instructions regarding War Diaries and Intelligence Summaries are contained in F. S. Regs., Part II. and the Staff Manual respectively. Title pages will be prepared in manuscript.

WAR DIARY

or

[redacted]

(*Erase heading not required.*)

Army Form C. 2118.

SEPTEMBER. 1918.

Place	Date	Hour	Summary of Events and Information	Remarks and references to Appendices
Sheet 57c	1/40,000			
MANANCOURT	20th		Rest day. a/C.S.M Jackson accidentally wounded.	
	21st		No1 Sec work on baths at ETRICOURT, No2 Sec baths at LE MESNIL, No3 Sec in Camp No4 C.R.E's Camp.	
	22nd		Sunday. Rest day. No2 Sec carry on work at baths at LE MESNIL.	
	23rd		Work the same as on 21st Sept.	
	24th		Work as before. In addition 1 hrs drill before work for No2 Sec. No 1, 3 & 4 sec only employ a few men, the remainder drill & training.	
HEUDECOURT W.8.d.3.4.	25th		Take over from 77th & 78th Field Coys R.E. No 1 & 2 Secs attached for work to 62nd Inf Bde. No 3 & 4 to 110th Inf Bde. No 3 & 4 sec work on Barricades in road W.6.d.6.2. to cover Battalion Hdqts from observation from GOUZEAUCOURT. Transport remains at MANANCOURT	
	26th		No 3 & 4 Sec work as before. No 1 & 2. work on Strong points commenced by 77th Field Coys at Q.34.d.5.58 – Q.34c. 6.1.	
	27th		No 3 & 4 complete barricades. No 1 & 2. proceed to put barricade across sunken road at Q.35a.8.80 block in trench at Q.29c. 9.7. captured that day. Enemy recaptured trench so block made at Q.35a.6.6.	
	29th		Orders received at 3am. to be prepared to bridge ESCAUT CANAL. The whole company attached to 110th Inf Bde. No 4 Sec under Lt STOCKDALE with 2nd Lt CULLIS as reconnaissance officer placed at disposal of Infantry for initial crossing. Remainder of company prepared to construct further	

A6945 Wt. W11422/M1160 350,000 12/16 D. D. & L. Forms/C./2118/14.

Instructions regarding War Diaries and Intelligence Summaries are contained in F. S. Regs., Par. II. and the Staff Manual respectively. Title pages will be prepared in manuscript.

WAR DIARY

or

[redacted].

(*Erase heading not required.*)

Army Form C. 2118.

SEPTEMBER 1918.

Place	Date	Hour	Summary of Events and Information	Remarks and references to Appendices
Sheet 57c	1/40,000			
HEUDECOURT.	29th		footbridges and one artillery bridge after initial crossing. Transport moves to P.36.d.5.9.	
			Major Campbell returns from leave.	
	30th		Transport rejoins Company. Lt Stockdale, 2/Lt Cullis & No 4 Sec move up to X.5.a.5.5	
			Remainder of company stand by. 1 Pontoon & 1 S.S. Wagon from No 3 Pontoon Park loaded with cork piers & trench gratings, & 4 pontoon wagons ready with bridging	
			equipment.	

M. H. Campbell
Maj R.E.
OC 95 Fd Coy R.E.

A6945 Wt. W11422/M1160 350,000 12/16 D. D. & L. Forms/C./2118/14.

CONFIDENTIAL Original

98TH
FIELD COMPANY,
R.E.
No. 75828
Date 1-11-18.

WAR DIARY

OF

98TH FIELD COY R.E.

FROM 1ST OCTOBER 1918. TO 31ST OCTOBER 1918.

VOLUME 37

Instructions regarding War Diaries and Intelligence Summaries are contained in F. S. Regs., Part II, and the Staff Manual respectively. Title pages will be prepared in manuscript.

WAR DIARY
or
INTELLIGENCE SUMMARY.
(Erase heading not required.)

Army Form C. 2118.

Vol 38

OCTOBER 1918.

Place	Date	Hour	Summary of Events and Information	Remarks and references to Appendices
Sheet 57c S.E. Heudecourt	1		Coy standing by for bridging of Canal de St. Quentin. Orders at night to take up material to Bantouzelle for a 20 ft Standard Bridge over Lock: then changed to a bridge for infantry in fours, made of 4 - 22' R.S.J. (12"x5"), with chesses as flooring. Lock is double, with one span 5 metres 50, the other 6 metres. Capt. McLaren took down 5 pontoons & 6 G.S. wagons, with 2 sections Rt. to assist, & unloaded at R 30 c. 6. 3, in front line. Gouzeaucourt-Bantouzelle Road not been worked on & very bad.	
	2		Coy still standing by - a number of canvas punts made, to hold 3 or 4 men. Orders for material for a second bridge over Lock to be taken down tonight to Bantouzelle - successfully accomplished by Capt McLaren. A number of cork floats also taken down.	
	3		Orders at 6 pm to get in touch with 110th Inf Bde to raft patrols across canal, but this scheme postponed. 2 sections improving 110th Bde Hdqrs in Quarry R 31 c 7. 7 during day.	
	4		Called on 110th Bde, & decided to carry floats, boats etc. close to W. bank of canal tonight, about M 31 b 3. 7 (Sheet 57b S.W.). For this purpose, a foot bridge over a 25' ditch immediately W. of Canal bank was made by No. 1 section, starting 10 pm. Considerable interference from snipers on E. bank of canal, also much shelling. Bridge completed by 03.00 hrs. 5th.	
	5		No. 4 section (forward section) carried rafts & tackle to above place. Lt Cullis, RE as reconnaissance officer carried out patrols during last few days & nights with infantry to obtain information about bridges, but was on no occasion able to reach canal.	

A6945 Wt. W11422/M1160 350,000 12/16 D. D. & L. Forms/C./2118/14.

Instructions regarding War Diaries and Intelligence Summaries are contained in F. S. Regs., Part II. and the Staff Manual respectively. Title pages will be prepared in manuscript.

WAR DIARY
or
~~INTELLIGENCE SUMMARY.~~
(*Erase heading not required.*)

Army Form C. 2118.

OCTOBER 1918

Place	Date	Hour	Summary of Events and Information	Remarks and references to Appendices
Sheet 57c S.E. 1/20,000.				
	5	11.00	Information from 110th Inf Bde that enemy retiring & troops crossed canal about 09.00 hrs on remains of demolished enemy bridges. No 1 sec started work 09.00 hrs on repair of bridge for infantry in file & bridge for infantry in fours about R36c9.9. No 2, 3 & 4 secs reached Bantouzelle Lock 14.00 hrs & started on one bridge for 1st Line Transport & 1 bridge for infantry in fours over Lock, also repair of demolished transport bridge over River Escaut at M26c 0.6 (57B S.W.). All bridges complete at 18.00 hrs, & 2 batteries R.F.A. over by 18.30 hrs. 5 R.S.J. per span used in transport bridge & 3 R.S.J. per span in infantry bridge. No enemy interference. Weather fine.	
R34d8.6	6.		Coy moved in morning to R34d8.6. Worked in afternoon on converting infantry bridge over Lock to bridge for 1st Line Transport by adding 2 R.S.J. per span & replaced chesses on this bridge by double thickness 2" planking salved from derelict bridges. Pontoon bridge across R. Escaut immediately S. of road bridge also made for infantry.	
	7.		Work on improving approaches to bridges. Warning order from C.R.E. 17.00 hrs that Coy to be held in readiness for work under 110th Inf Bde. Orders from Bde 19.30 hrs for 4 secs to be at road junction N31a2.5 at 23.00 hrs for work with 2 battalions on consolidation & cutting gaps in wire. Pitch black night & roads blocked; coy reached rendezvous 23.30 hrs, but battalions did not arrive till 00.45 hrs. (8th).	

A6945 Wt. W11422/M1160 350,000 12/16 D. D. & L. Forms/C./2118/14.

Instructions regarding War Diaries and Intelligence Summaries are contained in F. S. Regs., Part II, and the Staff Manual respectively. Title pages will be prepared in manuscript.

WAR DIARY

~~or~~

~~INTELLIGENCE SUMMARY.~~

(*Erase heading not required.*)

Army Form C. 2118.

OCTOBER 1918

Place	Date	Hour	Summary of Events and Information	Remarks and references to Appendices
Sheet 57B S.W. 1/20,000				
	8		1st Zero for attack 01.00 hrs, after which 2 secs proceeded to cut gaps in wire for 500 yds N of road at N.32.c.0.5, to assist in assembly for Bns for second attack starting 05.00 hrs. 2 secs allotted to these Bns & made strong pts near Maleassise Copse, N.21.c.2.5 & near Haut Farm, N.27.c. Events proved folly of attaching sections R.E. to battalions for consolidation purposes as they get sent forward too soon, & O.C. Fd Coy has no control over them. Sections returned to camp 18.00 hrs. Lt. F.H.G. Stockdale, R.E. wounded; 1 O.R. killed & 13 O.R. wounded. 4 O.R. missing.	
	9		Sections resting in morning & working on roads around Bertouzelle in afternoon.	
Guillemin	10		Coy moved 09.30 hrs to new camp at Guillemin Farm, N.17.a.9.5.	
	11		Coy cleaning up & resting. Collected bridging equipment (both spare & Inf. Bridge) from Bertry, & made Coy Equipment up to strength.	
	12		1 section erecting baths for 110th Inf. Bde at Caullery; 3 N.C.O.s & 3 men attached to 110th Bde for purposes of detection & destruction of Booby Traps.	
Walincourt	13		Coy moved to billets in Walincourt. Very good quarters in empty houses.	
	14		Training in morning – drill, musketry, physical training – & cleaning up in afternoon.	
	15		1 section to 110th Inf Bde for making targets; rest of coy. training as before. 2nd Lt. W.H. Cullis, R.E. evacuated "Sick".	

Instructions regarding War Diaries and Intelligence Summaries are contained in F. S. Regs., Part II. and the Staff Manual respectively. Title pages will be prepared in manuscript.

WAR DIARY
~~or~~
~~INTELLIGENCE SUMMARY.~~
(Erase heading not required.)

Army Form C. 2118.

OCTOBER, 1918

Place	Date	Hour	Summary of Events and Information	Remarks and references to Appendices
Sheet 57B.				
Walincourt	16.		Training in morning – drill & technical. 25 men inoculated	
	17 & 18.		Training as before. 30 men inoculated. Weather unsettled	
	19		Major Campbell went on leave. 15 men inoculated. Training as before	
	20		Rest day	
	21		Training and sports. No3 Sec. under 2/Lt. J. H. St. Johnston proceed at 1700 hours to join 110th Inf. Bde to assist infantry in crossing streams etc during an advance. This section stayed at CAULLERY.	
	22		Remainder of Company proceed to AUDENCOURT. Only 40 men billet, remainder in Bivouacs. No3 Sec moved	
AUDENCOURT			to Quarry at J.16.d 5.8 near INCHY. Here they were attached to 6th Bn Leics Regt & moved in front of NEUVILLY	
Sheet 57B " 51A " 51.	23		Battle commenced. No3 Sec advanced to OVILLERS at 0500 hours. At 11.30 hours they moved down to River HARPIES at VENDIGIES-AU-BOIS. They constructed 5 Infantry footbridges & removed charges from two brick arch bridges. They also constructed an approach to one of these bridges. This section rejoined the	
NEUVILLY			company at 19.30 hours. At 12.15 hours the remainder of the company moved to NEUVILLY. 19.30 hours three sections proceed to dig strong points in front of VENDIGIES-AU-BOIS at F1.d.8.9 F.2.c.7.8 & F.8.a.6.9. These sections returned at 03.00 hours to NEUVILLY.	
OVILLERS	24.		12.00 hours No3 Sec move to VENDIGIES-AU-BOIS. 13.30 Sections with transport move to OVILLERS. Horses return to NEUVILLY. 17.30 Three sections proceeded to dig strong points in front of POIX-DU-NORD at	

A6945 Wt. W11422/M1160 350,000 12/16 D. D. & L. Forms/C./2118/14.

Army Form C. 2118.

Instructions regarding War Diaries and Intelligence Summaries are contained in F. S. Regs., Part II. and the Staff Manual respectively. Title pages will be prepared in manuscript.

WAR DIARY
or
~~INTELLIGENCE SUMMARY.~~
(Erase heading not required.)

OCTOBER 1918

Place	Date	Hour	Summary of Events and Information	Remarks and references to Appendices
Sheet 57 B / " 51 A				
OVILLERS	24		at X 28.d., X.29.a, X23d & X24.c. Two platoons 14. North. Fus (P) wired these points. No3 Sec investigate mines.	
	25		Three sections & 1 platoon 14th N.F (P) wired 7 strong points constructed by 126th Field Coy. RE in X17 & X.22. No3 Sec repaired bridges & roads.	
NEUVILLY.	26		14.00 Three sections returned to old billets at NEUVILLY. No3 Sec made Bde Hdqts at OVILLERS. Total casualties during battle 1 Lt. D. M. MENZIES (wounded at duty), 2.O.R. killed, 3 O.R. wounded, 2.O.R. wounded gassed.	
	27		No1 Sec construct ramp in Quarry at OVILLERS to assist a tank which had fallen in to get out. No2 & 4 Sections rest. No 3 Sec return to Company.	
	28		No2 Sec carry on work for Tank. No3 Sec repair roads in village. No4 Sec salve wire. No1 Sec rest.	
VENDIGIES–	29		16.00 Hours Company moved to VENDIGIES-AU-BOIS.	
AU–BOIS.	30		No4 Sec under 1 Lt. E.F. MOLONY attached to 110th Inf Bde & move to POIX-DU-NORD & work on Front line & Brigade Hdqts. Lt HARDEN with 200 Pioneers commences work on Assembly Trenches 500 yards from front line & parallel to them in stretches of 150 yds trench, 150 yards gap. Remainder of company improving existing Strong Points.	
	31		Work carried on as on 30th.	

W. R. F. McLaren
Capt. R.E.

a/O.C. 98th Field Coy R.E.

A6945 Wt. W11422/M1160 350,000 12/16 D. D. & L. Forms/C./2118/14.

CONFIDENTIAL

V.R. 39

WAR DIARY

OF

98TH FIELD COY. RE

FROM 1ST NOV 1918 TO 30TH NOV. 1918

VOLUME 39

Instructions regarding War Diaries and Intelligence Summaries are contained in F. S. Regs., Part II. and the Staff Manual respectively. Title pages will be prepared in manuscript.

WAR DIARY
or
~~INTELLIGENCE SUMMARY~~

(Erase heading not required.)

Army Form C. 2118.

NOVEMBER.

Place	Date	Hour	Summary of Events and Information	Remarks and references to Appendices
Sheets 57 B. 51 A. 51.				
	1st		No 4 Sec attached to 110th Inf Bde & live in POIX-DU-NORD. Work on Bde & 7th Battn Leicestershire Regt Hdqts.	Lt. E.F.
VENDEGIES-AU-BOIS.			MOLONY supervised work on a new front line system of trenches along GHISSIGNIES-ENGLEFONTAINE road dug by infantry.	
			Lt. J.E. HARBEN with Pioneer working parties constructed assembly trenches parallel to this road. Remainder of company assisted in this work.	
	2nd		Division relieved. Company moved from billets in village to the CHATEAU. No 4 Sec return to company. Assembly trenches completed.	
	3rd		Rest day. Horse lines shelled by long range gun.	
	4th		X Corps attack. No 2 Sec attached to 110th Inf Bde for parapeting trenches. No 3 Sec under O.C. 97th Field Coy marched to FUTOY to repair JOLIMETZ-LOCQUIGNOL road. Company moved to POIX-DU-NORD.	
POIX-DU-NORD	5th		No 1 & No 4 Sec were attached to 6th Battn LEICS. & 1st Battn WILTS to assist in advance. No 2 & 3 sections attached to 110th Inf Bde. Sappers moved off at 0300 hours. No 1 & 4 cleared tracks & remained with infantry in LA TETE NOIRE. No 2 & 3 made two tracks with 126th Field Coy. R.E. mended crater at LA TETE NOIRE. Transport moved to LOCQUIGNOL. No 2 & 3 Sec got in at 20,00 hours.	
LOCQUIGNOL	6th		No 1 & 4 Sec helped Infantry to cross SAMBRE & removed mines in existing bridges. They were then employed on demolition around craters at BERLAIMONT. No 2 & 3 Sec under 126th Field Coy R.E. made 1st line Transport bridge over SAMBRE Lock at BERLAIMONT out of material on the spot. Transport moved to LA TETE NOIRE	

A6945 Wt. W11422/M1160 350,000 12/16 D. D. & L. Forms/C./2118/14.

Instructions regarding War Diaries and Intelligence Summaries are contained in F. S. Regs., Part II. and the Staff Manual respectively. Title pages will be prepared in manuscript.

WAR DIARY
or
~~INTELLIGENCE SUMMARY.~~
(Erase heading not required.)

Army Form C. 2118.

NOVEMBER.

Place	Date	Hour	Summary of Events and Information	Remarks and references to Appendices
Sheet 51.				
LA TETE NOIRE	7th		No 1 & 4 sec put culvert in crater at BERLAIMONT & commence to fill it in. No 2 & 3 sec under 126th Field Coy	
			R.E. complete Trestle bridge across SAMBRE commenced by 126th Field Coy, during the night.	
"	8th		Crater at BERLAIMONT ready for single lorry transport traffic at 10.00 hours. Major Campbell	
			returns from leave. Lt Lyne, RE reported for duty, but transferred by C.R.E. to 97 Fd Coy RE	
	9th		Rest day except for few men on upkeep of roadway over crater. Casualties during battle. 6 O.R. wounded.	
	10th		Sections working on road repair in Berlaimont. Section of Sambre Canal,	
			immediately North of destroyed bridge at W17b3.9, taken for C.E. V Corps.	
	11th		Orders received 0100 hrs for coy. to move with 110th Inf Bde to relieve 52nd Bde at	
			Beaufort. Orders received 09.00 hrs that "Hostilities will cease 11.00 hrs."	
			Coy moved off 12.30 hrs via Aulnoye, Limont Fontaine to Ropsies (W16c), where	
Ropsies W16c.			outpost coy of 110th Bde also billetted	
	12.		O.C. attended Conference at 110th Bde H.Q. Probably remaining in present billets for	
			25 days & then moving forward to Germany. General smartening up to be carried out.	
Damousies	13.		Company moved to good billets in Damousies, for work on craters at W18d5.2,	
			& W7a.9.0.	
Sheet 52	14.		Work commenced on repair of craters. O.C. on reconnaissance in afternoon	
Cousolre. M30.			with C.R.E. to destroyed bridge at Cousolre, & company moved there at night.	

A6945 Wt. W11422/M1160 350,000 12/16 D. D. & L. Forms/C./2118/14.

Instructions regarding War Diaries and Intelligence Summaries are contained in F. S. Regs., Part II. and the Staff Manual respectively. Title pages will be prepared in manuscript.

WAR DIARY

or

~~INTELLIGENCE SUMMARY.~~

(Erase heading not required.)

Army Form C. 2118.

NOVEMBER, 1918.

Place	Date	Hour	Summary of Events and Information	Remarks and references to Appendices
Sheet 52.				
Cousolre.	15th		Bridge to be prepared at M.30a.5.0. – total span about 45' from bank to bank.	
			All material to be carted from German Bridging dump at Malpert G25b. 4 trestles	
			[illegible] of 12"x12" timber & road bearers to be 8"x8". Bridge to take up to 12 ton axle load	
			& to be finished by early morning of 17th, to allow advancing Army to cross.	
	16.		Work continued on bridge: two sections 126th Fd Coy R.E. allotted for work on bridge, & 2 lorries for carting. Bridge completed by 23.59 hrs. Foggy weather.	
Sheet 51. Ferrière-la-Petite	17		Company moved back to good billets at Ferrière-la-Petite	
	18		Rest day, baths & cleaning up.	
	19–20		Working on crater at Obrechies: completed for 5 ton axle load.	
Berlaimont	21		Company moved to billets in Berlaimont. Lt. E.F. Molony R.E. on leave to U.K.	
	22–28		Cleaning up, training, sports & salving.	
	29.		Work as before. 3 coal miners despatched for interview, & if suitable, being sent straight to U.K. 4 Military Medals awarded to men of coy. for bridging of Sambre.	
	30.		Transport of coy, with that of 97th & 126th Fd Coys R.E., all under Capt. [illegible], 9 days [illegible] moved off 9.00 hrs for Neuilly, en route for Amiens Area. Dismounted personnel to move on Dec 1st.	
Ref. Valenciennes 1/100,000.				

[illegible signature]
OC 96th Fd Coy R.E.

A6945 Wt. W11422/M1160 350,000 12/16 D. D. & L. Forms/C./2118/14.

"A" Form.
Army Form C. 2121.
(In pads of 100.)

MESSAGES AND SIGNALS.

No. of Message ....

Prefix .... Code .... m. Office of Origin and Service Instructions.	Words. Charge. Sent At .... m. To .... By	This message is on a/c of: .... Service. (Signature of "Franking Officer.")	Recd. at ...... m. Date .... From .... By ....

TO CRE. 21st Div

Sender's Number.	Day of Month.	In reply to Number.	AAA
* F25	14	Ref. RE. 8303	

Certified that Copy No 24 of Code Calls issued on 4th August has been destroyed aaa

From 98th Fd Co. RE.
Place
Time

The above may be forwarded as now corrected. (Z)
.... Censor.
Signature of Addressor or person authorised to telegraph in his name. Maj. RE

*This line, except A A A, should be erased if not required.

Wt. W 3253/P511. 500,000 Pads. 1/18. B. & S. Ltd. (E2380.)

CONFIDENTIAL

WAR DIARY

OF

98TH FIELD COY RE

FROM. 1ST DECR 1918 TO 31ST DECR 1918

VOLUME 39.

98TH
FIELD COMPANY,
R.E.
No. 96352
Date 31-12-18

"A" Form.
MESSAGES AND SIGNALS.

Army Form C. 2121.
(In pads of 100.)
No. of Message ....

Prefix .... Code .... m. Office of Origin and Service Instructions.	Words.	Charge.	This message is on a/c of: .... Service. (Signature of "Franking Officer.")	Recd. at ...... m.
	Sent			Date ....
	At .... m.			From ....
	To			
	By			By ....

TO | C.R.E. | 21st | Division

Sender's Number.	Day of Month.	In reply to Number.	AAA
* F 24	14	S.P. 418	

Received

From 98th Fld Co. R.E.
Place
Time

Capt R.E.
for Maj R.E.

The above may be forwarded as now corrected.
(Z)
.... Censor.
Signature of Addressor or person authorised to telegraph in his name.

*This line, except **AAA**, should be erased if not required.

Wt. W 3253/P511. 500,000 Pads. 1/18. B. & S. Ltd. (E2389.)

C.E. 4/98

Instructions regarding War Diaries and Intelligence Summaries are contained in F. S. Regs., Part II. and the Staff Manual respectively. Title pages will be prepared in manuscript.

WAR DIARY
or
~~INTELLIGENCE SUMMARY.~~
(Erase heading not required.)

VR 40

Army Form C. 2118.

DECEMBER 1918

Place	Date	Hour	Summary of Events and Information	Remarks and references to Appendices
Valenciennes (1/100000)	1		Dismounted personnel moved off 0900 hrs by march route to Englefontaine, where parked for night with 97th & 126th Fd Coys R.E. H.M. The King drove through village about 16.00 hrs. Transport bought at Villers Outreaux. 2/Lt. J.H.S. Johnston awarded the M.C.	
	2		Moved off 0900 hrs to Salesches Stn, where entrained in empty supply train. Train started 1230 hrs. Transport bought at Tincourt (St. Quentin 1/100,000).	
Amiens (1/100000)	3		Arrived Amiens 0900 hrs. Lorry provided to carry blankets etc. Company marched to Bovelles, arriving 1500 hrs. Billets fairly good in an empty "Petit Chateau". Transport at Froyart.	
Bovelles	4		Coy settling down. CRE called with reference to provision of bunks or huts for all men in area who under existing arrangements are not sleeping on wood floors. This entails either huts or bunks being erected for practically every man in Bde Group (110th). Accomodation very bad, dilapidated & dirty on the whole. Transport at G[illegible].	
	5		Transport arrived 1300 hrs: no casualties en route. Lt. Harber RE to HQ RE to be acting Adjutant.	
	6th		Practically no work done owing to scarcity of material. No huts yet arrived.	
	7th		Small Nissen Huts began to arrive, & work started at Guignemicourt.	
	8th–11th		Work as before. 10th/2/Lt. E.F. Molony returned from leave.	
	12th		No[illegible]. Started work on hutting at Clairy. Weather very rainy.	

A6945 Wt. W11422/M1160 350,000 12/16 D. D. & L. Forms/C./2118/14.

Instructions regarding War Diaries and Intelligence Summaries are contained in F. S. Regs., Part II. and the Staff Manual respectively. Title pages will be prepared in manuscript.

WAR DIARY
~~INTELLIGENCE SUMMARY.~~
(Erase heading not required.)

Army Form C. 2118.

DECEMBER 1918.

Place	Date	Hour	Summary of Events and Information	Remarks and references to Appendices
Amiens (1/100,000)				
BOVELLES	13th-14th		Work on hutting as before. 14th Lt D. M. Menzies returned from leave to U.K.	
	15th		Rest day & baths.	
	16th-19th		Work as usual. 17th 100th Bde Group arrived in area.	
	20th		Supply of huts increased, & more transport available. Started work in Ferrières (No 1 sec) & Argoeuves (No 2 sec).	
	21st-24th		Work as usual. Weather extremely unsettled. 22nd Lt J. H. St Johnston, on leave to U.K.	
	25th-26th		Christmas holidays. A.F.Z.16 completed for whole coy. 5 coal miners departed for U.K.	
	27th-31st		Work as before. 3 men on courses at Army Workshops (2 fitting, 1 tinsmith).	
			Hutting situation: Guignemicourt: 1 large huts & 2 small huts. Complete	
			Clairy : 1 — — & 11 — — —	
			Ferrières : 1 — — & 7 — — —	
			St Sauveur : 1 — — —	
			Argoeuves : 10 — — —	
	29		Lt J. E. Harben on leave to U.K.	
	28		O.C., Capt McLaren & Sgt W. H. Graham "Mentioned".	

[signature] Capt. for Major R.E.
O.C. 98th Fd Coy R.E.

9

Adjutant

Please deal with these

G

1.2.19.

98 41

21 Div

Confidential.

WAR DIARY

of

98th Field Coy RE

From 1/1/19 to 31/1/19

Vol 40

Instructions regarding War Diaries and Intelligence Summaries are contained in F. S. Regs., Part II. and the Staff Manual respectively. Title pages will be prepared in manuscript.

WAR DIARY
~~or~~
~~INTELLIGENCE SUMMARY.~~
(Erase heading not required.)

Army Form C. 2118.

JANUARY 1919

Place	Date	Hour	Summary of Events and Information	Remarks and references to Appendices
Amiens 1/100,000				
BOVELLES	1		Work in morning, owing to urgent need of huts. Holiday in afternoon	
	2		Hutting work at Oissy, Guignemicourt, Ferrieres, Ailly-s-Somme, St Sauveur, Argoeuves	
			Lt. Brounger RE, reported for duty from 410th Fd Coy RE.	
	3-4		Work as usual. C.S.M. Jackson, of this unit, awarded D.C.M.	
	5		Rest day. Weather very rainy.	
	6-11		Work on hutting as usual. Supply of huts decreased & work somewhat delayed	
			Men demobilized: 11th 9 O.R. 6th Capt. H.P.L. Nelson on leave to U.K. 7th 2Lt J.H. St Aubyn returned from leave to U.K. 8th 2Lt W.H. Callis RE rejoined for duty from hospital	
	12		Rest day, baths & sports.	
	13-18		Hutting as before: need of huts disappeared & about 40 in area are unoccupied.	
	15th		G.O.C. 21st Div. addressed company in afternoon.	
			Demobilization: 12th 3 O.R.: 13th 7 O.R.: 19th 1 officer (Lt Brounger) & 3 O.R.	
	18th		Horses been classified by D.A.D.V.S. into Groups A, B, C or D, & by Remount Officer into Groups X, Y, or Z.	
	19th		Rest day, baths & sports. 2Lt W.H. Callis, on leave to U.K. Weather improved & colder	
	20-25		Hutting as before. Hutting requirements now cut down to what is actually needed	

A6945 Wt. W11422/M1160 350,000 12/16 D. D. & L. Forms/C./2118/14.

Instructions regarding War Diaries and Intelligence Summaries are contained in F. S. Regs., Part II. and the Staff Manual respectively. Title pages will be prepared in manuscript.

WAR DIARY
or
~~INTELLIGENCE SUMMARY.~~
(*Erase heading not required.*)

Army Form C. 2118.

JANUARY 1919

Place	Date	Hour	Summary of Events and Information	Remarks and references to Appendices
Amiens 1/100,000				
Bovelles	20-25		Demobilization: - 21st 12 O.R.: 25th 1 officer (2/Lt Menzies, M.C.) + 10 O.R.	
	23rd		Capt. W.P.F. McLaren returned from leave to U.K.	
	26th		Holiday, battle & sports. First fall of snow today.	
	27-31st		Hutting work as before. About 20 men available for this now.	
	"		Demobilization: 27th - 12 horses (of Y group): 28th - 8 O.R.: 29th - 7 O.R.	
	1-31st		Total demobilization for month: 2 officers, 56 O.R., 12 horses. Majority of O.R. came from Group 30 (Building & construction trades).	
			Total huts erected to end of month	
			Clairy - 1 Hospital Nissen, 1 Standard 60'x16', 25 Small Nissen	
			Guignemicourt - 2 Hospital Nissen, 40 Small Nissen	
			Ferrières - 3 Hospital Nissen, 14 Small Nissen	
			Bovelles - 3 small Nissen	
			Argœuves - 1 Hospital Nissen, 23 Small Nissen	
			St Sauveur - 7 small Nissen. Ailly - 5 Small Nissen. Dreuil - 1 small Nissen	
			Montières - 4 small Nissen	
			TOTAL: 7 Hospital Nissen, 1 Standard, 122 Small Nissen	

[illegible signature] Major
O.C. 98th Fd Coy R.E.?

A6945 Wt. W11422/M1160 350,000 12/16 D. D. & L. Forms/C./2118/14.

98 4 21/2

CONFIDENTIAL

WAR DIARY

OF

98TH FIELD COMPANY R.E.

FROM 1ST FEB 1919. TO 28TH FEB. 1919

VOLUME. 41.

98TH
FIELD COMPANY,
R.E.
No. G 7240
Date 1.3.19.

Instructions regarding War Diaries and Intelligence Summaries are contained in F. S. Regs., Part II. and the Staff Manual respectively. Title pages will be prepared in manuscript.

WAR DIARY
~~or~~
~~INTELLIGENCE SUMMARY.~~
(*Erase heading not required.*)

Army Form C. 2118.

FEBRUARY, 1919

Place	Date	Hour	Summary of Events and Information	Remarks and references to Appendices
AMIENS	1/100,000			
BOVELLES	1st–4th		Nothing much in progress at Ailly-s-Somme & St. Sauveur only.	
	2nd		Conference at Hdqrs. RE with regard to construction of new camp at Dreuil of 50 huts required owing to re-adjustment of Divisional area. All available sappers from 97th & 126th Fd Coys to work with 98th Coy on the job – total labour about 50 men.	
	4th		2 officers & 22 O.R. compulsorily retained under A.O. 55 of 1919 for armies of occupation.	
	5th–8th		Work on new camp at Dreuil – actual erection started on 6th. Weather cold.	
	7th		Coy attended concert by R.E. Band at Bougainville in afternoon.	
	9th		Rest day.	
	10th		Work at Dreuil Camp stopped – camp no longer required. 20 huts erected & 28 lying on site.	
	11th		Detachments from other companies returned to respective Coy Hdqrs.	
			II Lt. W.H. Cutler R.E. returned from leave.	
	12th–15th		Sappers working on cleaning up of tools, equipment etc.	
	16		Rest day. Weather very unsettled.	
	17th–21st		Work on cleaning up.	
	22		6 O.R. detached for work under 97 Coy R.E. on Cadre Camp.	
			Company now 2 above Cadre B strength. Forced to retain 17 men on Cadre, who are otherwise available for Army of Occupation.	

A6945 Wt. W11422/M1160 350,000 12/16 D. D. & L. Forms/C./2118/14.

Army Form C. 2118.

Instructions regarding War Diaries and Intelligence Summaries are contained in F. S. Regs., Part II. and the Staff Manual respectively. Title pages will be prepared in manuscript.

WAR DIARY
~~or~~
INTELLIGENCE ~~SUMMARY.~~
(Erase heading not required.)

FEBRUARY 1919

Place	Date	Hour	Summary of Events and Information	Remarks and references to Appendices
Amiens 1/100,000				
Borellus	23-28		Work as usual. A.O. III of 28th [illegible] published authorising grant of bonus to all personnel in Cadres, as part of Machinery of Demobilization	
	24		15 "Z" horses despatched to Forges-les-Eaux. All horses surplus to actual requirements withdrawn to date.	
	Total		Demobilization for Month:—	
			1st - 9 O.R.: 2nd - 4 O.R.: 6th - 1 officer (Lt. E.F. Malony) & 12 O.R.: 9th - 6 O.R.: 13th - 7 O.R.	
			16th - 3 O.R.: 20th - 6 O.R.: 23rd - 1 O.R.: 27th - 1 O.R. Total - 1 officer, 49 O.R.	
			Horses Despatched 4th - 6 (X): 24th - 16 (Z): Remaining on strength 26 Z + 11 X horses	
	Total		Hutting for Month:—	
			Clary - 1 small Nissen: St Sauveur - 5 small Nissen	
			Pilly - 5 small Nissen: Saveuse - 3 small Nissen	
			Dreuil - 20 small Nissen	

[signature]
Major R.E.
O.C. 98 Fd Coy R.E.

10

98 Fld Co RE

21

Army Form C. 2118.

Instructions regarding War Diaries and Intelligence Summaries are contained in F. S. Regs., Part II. and the Staff Manual respectively. Title pages will be prepared in manuscript.

WAR DIARY
or
~~INTELLIGENCE SUMMARY.~~
(Erase heading not required.)

MARCH 1919

43

Place	Date	Hour	Summary of Events and Information	Remarks and references to Appendices
Amiens 1/100,000				
Borettes	1		Work on cleaning up stores & wagons	
	2		Summer time in force from night 1st/2nd. Instructions received to send wagons to Cadre Park at Longpré near Amiens.	
	3		2 Pontoon & 1 Trestle wagons sent to Cadre Park, with 2 men as storemen. 9 Z horses demobilized today via Hornoy.	
	4		Conference at CRE's in afternoon re closing up of the Coys. Decided that 98 Coy should move to Oissy (97 Coy RE billets) on Thursday.	
	5.		1 Tool cart, 2½ limbers, 1 G.S. wagon, 1 Mess cart & 1 Water cart sent to Cadre Park today. 12 Z horses demobilized for sale in Amiens.	
	6.		10 horses lent to 126th Coy to assist moving their wagons to Cadre Park. Coy moved to Oissy. Lorry provided for kit etc. 1 Z rider demobilized. 2 [illegible] Details dispatched to U.K. Horses feeling effects of 14 mile journey to Longpré.	
OISSY	7.		1 N.C.O sent to DREUIL to take charge of party of Pioneers dismantling & loading huts for use in Cadre Camp. All X horses & mules malleined.	
	8.		Lt. CALLIS proceeds on leave in France.	

Instructions regarding War Diaries and Intelligence Summaries are contained in F. S. Regs., Part II. and the Staff Manual respectively. Title pages will be prepared in manuscript.

WAR DIARY
or
~~INTELLIGENCE SUMMARY.~~
(Erase heading not required.)

Army Form C. 2118.

MARCH. 1919.

Place	Date	Hour	Summary of Events and Information	Remarks and references to Appendices
AMIENS 1/100,000				
OISSY	9.		MAJOR CAMPBELL proceeds on leave to ENGLAND. 1Y. Rider demobilized. 3 Tool Carts & 1½ limbers sent to Cadre Camp.	
	10		Supply S.S. Wagon handed over by No 3 Coy. Train.	
	11		Supply S.S Wagon sent to Cadre Camp. All company transport now at Cadre Camp.	
	12		N.C.O returns from DREUIL having dismantled 3 huts & loaded 14.	
	13.		7. Y.L.D horses demobilized.	
	14.		All bicycles handed in to 21st Div D.A.D.O.S. 2/Lt St JOHNSTON rejoined from Course.	
	15		Huts handed over to Area Commandant by Units vacating MONTIERES, GUIGNEMICOURT & CLAIRY checked.	
	16.		2/Lt. St JOHNSTON returns to No 2 School of Chemistry DOULLENS for a further course. 1.O.R. demobilized	
	17.		Hutting Complete at LONGPRE	
	19		2/Lt CALLIS returns from leave.	
	20.		C.Q.M.S proceeds to Cadre Camp to superintend checking & cleaning of Coy equipment preparatory to inspection by D.A.D.O.S 2/Lt St JOHNSTON. M.C. posted to 222nd (Field) Coy R.E. 2/Lt. C.G. CAROLIN.M.C transferred from 126th (Field) Coy RE to 98 (Field) Coy.	
	22		2/Lt CALLIS. posted to 222nd (Field) Coy RE.	
	25		14.O.R transferred to 438th Field Coy RE & 1.O.R to 529th Field Coy RE 3rd Division of the Rhine	

A6945 Wt. W11422/M1160 350,000 12/16 D. D. & L. Forms/C./2118/14.

Instructions regarding War Diaries and Intelligence Summaries are contained in F. S. Regs., Part II. and the Staff Manual respectively. Title pages will be prepared in manuscript.

WAR DIARY
or
~~INTELLIGENCE SUMMARY.~~
(Erase heading not required.)

Army Form C. 2118.

MARCH 1919

Place	Date	Hour	Summary of Events and Information	Remarks and references to Appendices
AMIENS	1/100,000			
OISSY	27		1. O.R. proceed to 438 (Field) Coy RE. Coy now down to Cadre "A" strength in men.	
			T/2nd Lt. C. S. CAROLIN. M.C. promoted Temp Lt. from 22nd Sept 1917.	
	28		3. X. Mules demobilised via BOURDON Camp.	
	28th–31st		Detachment at LONGPRÉ clean & adjust equipment. Remainder of Coy, sport & route marches.	
	31st		Coy 10 R understrength on Cadre establishment. Major Campbell surplus to Cadre.	
	1–31st		Demobilisation :– 3. O.R.	
			Transferred. – 2 Officers (2nd Lt. W.H. CULLIS + 2nd Lt J.H. ST. JOHNSTON M.C.) to 222nd Field Coy RE	
			:– 15. O.R to 438 Field Coy RE. 1 O.R to 529 Field Coy RE.	
			Horses & Mules :– 3 X mules demobilised; 8 Y. horses "; 13 Z " " } Total left. 4 Z horses	
			Hutting. 3 Huts dismantled at DREUIL & 14 load on lorries from DREUIL Camp.	
			W P [illegible] Capt RE a/O.C. 98th Field Coy RE	

Instructions regarding War Diaries and Intelligence Summaries are contained in F. S. Regs., Part II. and the Staff Manual respectively. Title pages will be prepared in manuscript.

WAR DIARY
or
~~INTELLIGENCE~~ SUMMARY.
(Erase heading not required.)

Army Form C. 2118.

MARCH 1919

Place	Date	Hour	Summary of Events and Information	Remarks and references to Appendices
AMIENS	1/100	000		
Orssy	27		1 O.R. proceeds to 438 (Field) Coy R.E. Coy now down to Cadre "A" strength in men. T/II Lt C.S. CAROLIN M.C. promoted Temp. Lt from 22nd Sept 1917	
	28		3 X mules demobilized via BOURDON Camp.	
	28–31		Detachment at LONGPRE cleaning + adjusting equipment. Remainder of Coy sport + route marches.	
	31		Coy. 1 O.R. understrength on Cadre establishment. Major CAMPBELL surplus to Cadre.	
	1–31		Demobilization 3 O.R.	
			Transferred – 2 Officers (II Lt. W.H. CULLIS + II Lt. J.H. St. JOHNSON M.C.) to 222nd Fld Coy RE – 15 O.R. to 438 Field Coy R.E. + 1 O.R. to 529 (Field) Coy RE	
			Horses + Mules – 3 X mules demobilized; 8 Y horses "; 13 Z " " } Total left 4 Z horses	
			Hutting – 3 Huts dismantled at DREUIL + 14 loaded in lorries from DREUIL Camp.	

Capt RE
a/O.C. 98 Field Coy. RE.

D. D. & L., London, E.C.
(10340) Wt W5300/P713 750,000 3/18 Sch. 52a Forms/C2118/16

Instructions regarding War Diaries and Intelligence Summaries are contained in F. S. Regs., Part II. and the Staff Manual respectively. Title pages will be prepared in manuscript.

WAR DIARY
or
~~INTELLIGENCE SUMMARY.~~
(Erase heading not required.)

Army Form C. 2118.

MARCH 1919.

Place	Date	Hour	Summary of Events and Information	Remarks and references to Appendices
AMIENS	1/100,000			
Bovelles	1		Work on cleaning up Stores + wagons	
	2		Summer time in force from night 1st/2nd Instructions received to send wagons to Cadre Park at LONGPRE near AIRAINES.	
	3		2 Pontoons + 1 Trestle wagons sent to Cadre Park, with 2 men as storemen. 9 Z horses demobilized today via HORNBY.	
	4		Conference at C.R.E. in afternoon reference closing up of Fld. Coys. Decided that 98 Coy should move to OISSY (97 Coy R.E. billets) on Thursday.	
	5		1 Toolcart, 2½ limbers, 1 G.S. wagon, 1 Mess Cart + 1 Water Cart sent to Cadre Park today. 12 Z horses demobilized for sale in AMIENS.	
	6		10 horses lent to 126 Fld Coy to assist moving their wagons to Cadre Park. Coy. moved to OISSY. lorry provided for Kit etc. 1 Z rider demobilized. 2 WATFORD details despatched to U.K.	
Oissy	7		Horses feeling effects of 14 mile journey to Longpre. 1 N.C.O. sent to DREUIL to take charge of party of Pioneers dismantling + loading huts for use in Cadre Camp. All X horses + mules malleined	
	8		2/Lt CULLIS proceeds on leave in FRANCE.	

D. D. & L., London, E.C.
(10340) Wt W5300/P713 750,000 3/18 E 1588 Forms/C2118/16

Army Form C. 2118.

Instructions regarding War Diaries and Intelligence Summaries are contained in F. S. Regs., Part II. and the Staff Manual respectively. Title pages will be prepared in manuscript.

WAR DIARY
or
~~INTELLIGENCE SUMMARY.~~
(Erase heading not required.)

MARCH 1919

Place	Date	Hour	Summary of Events and Information	Remarks and references to Appendices
AMIENS	1/100,000			
OISSY	9		Major CAMPBELL proceeds on leave to England. 1 Y Rider demobilized 3 Tool Carts + 1½ limbers sent to Cadre Camp.	
	10		Supply G.S. Wagon handed over by No 3 Coy. Train.	
	11		Supply G.S. Wagon send to Cadre Camp. All Company transport now at Cadre Camp.	
	12		N.C.O. returns from DREUIL having dismantled 3 huts + loaded 14.	
	13		7 Y L.D. horses demobilized	
	14		All bicycles handed in to 21st DIV. D.A.D.O.S. II Lt. St. JOHNSON rejoined from Course	
	15		Huts handed over to Area Commandant by Units vacating MONTIERES, GUIGNEMICOURT + CLAIRY checked.	
	16		II Lt. St JOHNSON returns to No 3 School of Chemistry DOULLENS for a further course. 1 O.R. demobilized.	
	17		Hutting complete at LONGPRE.	
	19		II Lt CULLIS returns from leave	
	20		C.Q.M.S proceeds to Cadre Camp to superintend checking + cleaning of Coy. equipment preparatory to inspection by D.A.D.O.S. II Lt. St JOHNSON M.C. posted to 222nd (Field) Coy R.E. II Lt. C.S. CAROLIN. M.C. transferred from 126 (Field) Coy. RE to 98 (Field) Coy.	
	22		II Lt. CULLIS posted to 222 (Field) Coy R.E.	
	25		11 O.R. transferred to 438 (Field) Coy RE + 1 O.R. to 529 (Field) Coy. RE 3rd Division of the Rhine	

D. D. & L., London, E.C.
(10340) Wt W5300/P713 750,000 3/18 E 2688 Forms/C2118/16

CONFIDENTIAL

VR 44

WAR DIARY

OF

98th FIELD COMPANY RE

FROM. 1st APR 1919 to 30th APR 1919.

Army Form C. 2118.

WAR DIARY

or

~~INTELLIGENCE SUMMARY.~~

(Erase heading not required.)

Instructions regarding War Diaries and Intelligence Summaries are contained in F. S. Regs., Part II. and the Staff Manual respectively. Title pages will be prepared in manuscript.

APRIL. 1918.

Place	Date	Hour	Summary of Events and Information	Remarks and references to Appendices
AMIENS	1/100,000			
OISSY	1st		2 Lt. J. H. St JOHNSTON M.C. Reported to 98th Field Coy.	
	1st-4th		Route Marches & sports.	
	4th		9.0 a.m. Coy moved to LE CATELET. M.T. allotted by division to move stores & blankets.	
LE CATELET	5th		Half day work at Cadre Camp LONGPRÈ cleaning & checking Harness. Cleaning Wagons	
	6th		Rest day 2 Horses & 2 Drivers attached 21st Div Signals to assist in collecting Cable in old Area.	
			Major W. L. Campbell returns from leave.	
	7th-9th		Work in Cadre Camp cleaning harness & wagons.	
	10th		Work continued in Cadre Camp. Major W. L. CAMPBELL proceeds to England for demobilization. 2 Lt	
			J. H. ST JOHNSTON M.C. posted to No 4 WORKSHOPS COY. R.E. ST. OUEN. 12 Horses demobilized.	
	11th		2 Z Horses transferred to 21st Div Signals RE. BOVELLES bath set removed to CONDE-FOLIE &	
			handed over to 126th Field Coy RE. Remainder of Coy at work in CADRE CAMP.	
	12th		Lt. G. G. CAROLIN returns from leave. Work suspended in Cadre Camp owing to bad weather.	
	13th		Rest day.	
	14th		98th Field Coy Office combined with C.R.E.'s office.	
	14-16		4 men per day at work in Cadre Camp. Remainder football etc.	
	16-23		4 men per day at work in Cadre. Most of the remainder on English or French leave.	

A6945 Wt. W11422/M1160 350,000 12/16 D. D. & L. Forms/C./2118/14.

Instructions regarding War Diaries and Intelligence Summaries are contained in F. S. Regs., Part II. and the Staff Manual respectively. Title pages will be prepared in manuscript.

WAR DIARY
or
~~INTELLIGENCE SUMMARY.~~
(Erase heading not required.)

Army Form C. 2118.

APRIL 1918

Place	Date	Hour	Summary of Events and Information	Remarks and references to Appendices
AMIENS 1/100,000				
LE CATELET	23rd		Inspection of Unserviceable equipment & A.F. G 1098 by A.D.O.S. Water cart condemned as Unserviceable	
(SOMME)	24th		Work in Cadre Camp. Extra guards arranged as establishment at Cadre Camp is	
	27th		reduced. Capt. McLean proceeds to U.K on leave.	
	28		1 OR proceeded for demobilisation	
	30		1 OR proceeded for demobilisation	

Charles Carolan Lieut RE
a/OC 98 Field Coy RE

A6945 Wt. W11422/M1160 350,000 12/16 D. D. & L. Forms/C./2118/14.

CONFIDENTIAL

VR 45

WAR DIARY

OF

98TH FIELD COMPANY R.E.

FROM 1ST MAY 1919 TO 31ST MAY 1919

VOLUME 44.

98TH
FIELD COMPANY,
R.E.
No. 97423.
Date

Instructions regarding War Diaries and Intelligence Summaries are contained in F. S. Regs., Part II. and the Staff Manual respectively. Title pages will be prepared in manuscript.

WAR DIARY
or
~~INTELLIGENCE SUMMARY.~~
(*Erase heading not required.*)

Army Form C. 2118.

MAY 1919.

Place	Date	Hour	Summary of Events and Information	Remarks and references to Appendices
AMIENS 1/100,000				
LE CATELET (Somme).	1st-31st		Men chiefly employed on guards at Cadre Camp LONGPRÉ. The remainder of the time was spent in sports.	
	10th		Lt C.S. CAROLIN. M.C. proceeded to England for Dispersal, Adj. R.E. acting O.C.	
	15		Capt. McLAREN returns from leave.	
	16		11. O.R. proceed to SAVEUSE Concentration Camp for Dispersal in U.K.	
	19th		Hdqts 21st Div. R.E. Cadre leaves for England.	
	24th		7. O.R. proceed to Concentration Camp for Dispersal in U.K.	
			W F McLaren Capt R.E. O.C. 98th Field Coy R.E.	

A5834 Wt. W4973/M687 750,000 8/16 D. D. & L. Ltd. Forms/C.2118/13.

21

V8 46

Ceased

CONFIDENTIAL

WAR DIARY

OF

98th FIELD COMPANY RE

FROM 1st June 1919 to 7th June 1919

Instructions regarding War Diaries and Intelligence Summaries are contained in F. S. Regs., Part II. and the Staff Manual respectively. Title pages will be prepared in manuscript.

Army Form C. 2118.

WAR DIARY
or
~~INTELLIGENCE SUMMARY.~~

98th Field Coy. RE (Erase heading not required.) June 1919.

Place	Date	Hour	Summary of Events and Information	Remarks and references to Appendices
LE CATELET (Somme)				
AMIENS 1/100,000.	1st		Orders received to disband unit.	
	2nd		Remaining Z horses transferred to 21st Div. Train. All wagons & equipment handed in to I.C.S. LONGPRE.	
	3rd		26 O.R proceeded to C.C.C. SAVEUSE for dispersal.	
	4th		Imprest Account closed.	
	7th		Capt McLAREN & 8 O.R proceed to C.C.C. CANDAS for dispersal	
			Unit completely disbanded.	

W P T McLaren
Capt RE
O.C. 98th Field Coy R.E.

A6945 Wt. W11422/M1160 350,000 12/16 D. D. & L. Forms/C./2118/14.

98th Field Coy R.E. (continued).

Rank.	Name.	Joined Unit.	Remarks.
Lieut.	E.L.V.DAKIN.	2.3.16.	Appointed A/Capt.29.11.16. Appointed A/Major 2.7.17. Promoted T/Capt.18.9.17. Awarded M.C.22.10.17. Mentioned in C.in C. Despatch 1.11.18. Wounded & Missing 22.3.18.
2/ Lieut.	W.L.CAMPBELL.	4.6.16.	Promoted T/Lt 1.1.16. Transferred to 126th Field Coy.28.9.17. Rejoined Unit 3.6.18. Appointed A/Major. 2.5.18.
2/Lt.	W.P.F.McLAREN	29.6.16.	Appointed T/Lt. 2.1.18. Appointed A/Capt.17.7.18. Wounded at duty 5.10.17.
Lieut.	A.WILLIAMSON.	27.11.16.	To 12th Fd.Coy.27.1.17.
2/Lt.	G.HEPBURN.	13.12.16.	Killed in action 22.3.18.
2/Lt.	W.T.SHAVER.	28.5.17.	Wounded 22.3.18.
2/Lt.	T.A.WOMERSLEY.	7.7.17.	Awarded M.C. 4.5.18. Wounded 27.5.18. Promoted T/Lt. 25.9.18.
Lieut.	G.F.C.BAILE.	11.10.17.	Transferred to 126th Fd. Coy.14.10.17.
2/Lt. *	T.K.McPHEE	14.12.17.	To Hospital 29.1.18.
2/Lt.	G.BOOTES.	17.4.18.	To 97th Fd.Coy.20.4.18.
2/Lt.	R.L.CADELL.	17.4.18.	Wounded and Missing 28.5.18.
2/Lt.	H.La BOYD-MOSS	17.4.18.	Wounded 27.5.18.
2/Lt.	R.M.KAY.	17.4.18.	To Hospital 30.5.18
2/Lt.	L.W.LILLINGSTON	18.6.18.	Gassed 21.8.18.
2/Lt.	D.M.MENZIES.	18.6.18.	Awarded M.C. 24.9.18. Wounded at duty 26.10.18.
2/Lt.	E.F.MOLONY.	25.6.18.	Wounded 21.8.18. Rejoined 12.10.18.
2/Lt.	R.W.HILLIER.	5.7.18.	Wounded 22.3.18.
Lieut.	W.J.VAUGHAN-WILLIAMS.	18.7.18.	To 105th Coy. R.E. 2.8.18.
Lieut.	J.E.HARBEN.	27.7.18.	

98th FIELD COMPANY R.E.

Rank.	Name	Joined Unit	Remarks.
Major.	C.COFFIN.	2.11.14.	Transferred to H.Q.21st Div R.E. 1.6.15.
2/Lt.	N.AYRIS.	2.11.14.	Promoted T/Lt.11.7.15. Killed in action 31/12/15
2/Lt.	G.A.GREGSON.	28.11.14.	Promoted T/Lt.11.7.15. Wounded 15.12.15. Rejoined 2.1.16. Wounded 24.2.16. Rejoined 13.2.17. Wounded 16.6.17. Rejoined 10.8.17. Promoted A/Capt.17.8.17. Promoted T/Capt.13.9.17. Transferred to R.A.F. 17.7.18.
2/Lt.	H.TAYLOR.	11.12.14.	Promoted T/Lt.11.7.15. Killed in action 27.2.16.
2/Lt.	M.H.SCHWAB.	11.12.14.	Promoted T/Lt.11.7.15. to 104 Fd. Coy.R.E.2nd in Command.
2/Lt.	G.E.LINES.	2.15.	To 126th Fd.Coy. 8.15.
Capt.	S.F.STOKES.	1.6.15.	Left Coy. about 13.8.15.
2/Lt.	A.W.METCALFE.	6.15.	Transferred to Newark 9.9.15.
Major	F.M.CLOSE.	22.6.15.	C.R.E. 14th Div.18.12.15.
Capt.	R.E.DEWING.	7.9.15.	Promoted A/Major on 18.12.15. to 17.1.16. Transferred to 223 Fd. Coy. 28.5.16.
Interpreter	R.M.G.BLONDEL.	9.9.18.	Transferred to H.Q R.E. 31.1.17. Awarded M.M. Nov 1916
Capt.	H.J.COUCHMAN.	19.12.15.	Promoted A/Major 19.12.15. Awarded M.C. 3.6.16. Promoted Major 25.11.16. Appointed C.R.E. 39th Div. 1.7.17.
2/Lt.	J.W.BULL.	3.1.16.	Died of wounds 25.9.16.
2/Lt.	F.HEWIN.	18.2.16.	Wounded 3.10.17. Awarded M.C. 23.10.17. Mentioned in C. in C. Despatch 1.1.18. Promoted 30.11.16. to T/Lt.

98th Field Coy. R.E. (continued).

Rank.	Name.	Joined Unit.	Remarks.
2/Lt.	J.H. ST. JOHNSTON	28.8.18.	Awarded M.C. 24.11.18.
2/Lt.	W.H. CULLIS.	13.9.18.	To Hospital 15.10.18. Rejoined 1.11.18. To Hospital 2.11.18.
2/Lt.	F.H.G. STOCKDALE.	19.9.18.	Wounded 8.10.18.
Lieut.	D.R. LYNE. M.C.,	10.11.18.	To 97th Fd.Coy. 14.11.18.
* ~~Capt.~~ LT.	A.H. SOUTAR. M.C.,	3.4.18.	Promoted A/Major 3.4.18. Wounded and Missing 28.5.18.

98th Field Coy. R.E. (continued).

Rank.	Name.	Joined Unit.	Remarks.
2/Lt.	J.H. ST. JOHNSTON	28.8.18.	Awarded M.C. 24.11.18.
2/Lt.	W.H. CULLIS.	13.9.18.	To Hospital 15.10.18. Rejoined 1.11.18. To Hospital 2.11.18.
2/Lt.	F.H.G. STOCKDALE.	19.9.18.	Wounded 8.10.18.
Lieut.	D.R. LYNE. M.C.,	10.11.18.	To 97th Fd.Coy. 14.11.18.
* ~~Capt.~~ LT.	A.H. SOUTAR. M.C.,	3.4.18.	Promoted A/Major 3.4.18. Wounded and Missing 28.5.18.

98th FIELD COMPANY R.E.

Rank.	Name	Joined Unit	Remarks.
Major.	C.COFFIN.	2.11.14.	Transferred to H.Q.21st Div R.E. 1.6.15.
2/Lt.	N.AYRIS.	2.11.14.	Promoted T/Lt.11.7.15. Killed in action 31/12/15
2/Lt.	G.A.GREGSON.	28.11.14.	Promoted T/Lt.11.7.15. Wounded 15.12.15. Rejoined 2.1.16. Wounded 24.2.16. Rejoined 13.2.17. Wounded 16.6.17. Rejoined 10.8.17. Promoted A/Capt.17.8.17. Promoted T/Capt.13.9.17. Transferred to R.A.F. 17.7.18.
2/Lt.	E.TAYLOR.	11.12.14.	Promoted T/Lt.11.7.15. Killed in action 27.2.16.
2/Lt.	M.H.SCHWAB.	11.12.14.	Promoted T/Lt.11.7.15. to 104 Fd. Coy.R.E.2nd in Command.
2/Lt.	G.E.LINES.	2.15.	To 126th Fd.Coy. 8.15.
Capt.	S.F.STOKES.	1.6.15.	Left Coy. about 13.8.15.
2/Lt.	A.W.METCALFE.	6.15.	Transferred to Newark 9.9.15.
Major	F.M.CLOSE.	22.6.15.	C.R.E. 14th Div.18.12.15.
Capt.	H.E.DEWING.	7.9.15.	Promoted A/Major on 18.12.15. to 17.1.16. Transferred to 223 Fd. Coy. 28.5.16.
Interpreter	R.M.G.BLONDEL.	9.9.18.	Transferred to H.Q R.E. 31.1.17. Awarded M.M. Nov 1916.
Capt.	H.J.COUGHMAN.	19.12.15.	Promoted A/Major 19.12.15. Awarded M.C. 3.6.16. Promoted Major 25.11.16. Appointed C.R.E. 39th Div. 1.7.17.
2/Lt.	J.W.BULL.	3.1.16.	Died of wounds 25.9.16.
2/Lt.	F.HEWIN.	18.2.16.	Wounded 3.10.17. Awarded M.C. 23.10.17. Mentioned in C. in C. Despatch 1.1.18. Promoted 30.11.16. to T/Lt.

98th Field Coy R.E. (continued).

Rank.	Name.	Joined Unit.	Remarks.
Lieut.	E.L.V.DAKIN.	2.3.16.	Appointed A/Capt.29.11.16. Appointed A/Major 2.7.17. Promoted T/Capt.18.9.17. Awarded M.C.22.10.17. Mentioned in C.in C. Despatch 111.18.Wounded & Missing 22.3.18. Promoted T/Lt 1.1.16.
2/Lieut.	W.L.CAMPBELL.	4.6.16.	Transferred to 126th Field Coy.28.9.17. Rejoined Unit 3.6.18. Appointed A/Major. 2.6.18.
2/Lt.	W.P.F.McLAREN	29.6.16.	Appointed T/Lt. 2.1.18. Appointed A/Capt.17.7.18. Wounded at duty 5.10.17.
Lieut.	A.WILLIAMSON.	27.11.16.	To 12th Fd.Coy.27.1.17.
2/Lt.	G.HEPBURN.	13.12.16.	Killed in action 22.3.18.
2/Lt.	W.T.SHAVER.	28.5.17.	Wounded 22.3.18.
2/Lt.	T.A.WOMERSLEY.	7.7.17.	Awarded M.C. 4.5.18. Wounded 27.5.18.Promoted T/Lt. 25.9.18.
Lieut.	G.F.C.BAILE.	11.10.17.	Transferred to 126th Fd. Coy.14.10.17.
2/Lt.	T.H.McPHEE	14.12.17.	To Hospital 29.1.18.
2/Lt. *	G.BOOTES.	17.4.18.	To 97th Fd.Coy.20.4.18.
2/Lt.	R.L.CADELL.	17.4.18.	Wounded and Missing 28.5.18.
2/Lt.	H.La BOYD-MOSS	17.4.18.	Wounded 27.5.18.
2/Lt.	R.M.KAY.	17.4.18.	To Hospital 30.5.18
2/Lt.	L.W.LILLINGSTON	18.6.18.	Gassed 21.8.18.
2/Lt.	D.M.MENZIES.	18.6.18.	Awarded M.C. 24.9.18. Wounded at duty 26.10.18.
2/Lt.	E.F.MOLONY.	25.6.18.	Wounded 21.8.18. Rejoined 12.10.18.
2/Lt.	H.W.HILLIER.	5.7.18.	Wounded 22.3.18.
Lieut.	W.J.VAUGHAN-WILLIAMS.	16.7.18.	To 105th Coy. R.E. 3.8.18.
Lieut.	J.E.HARBEN.	27.7.18.	

Rank.	Name.	Joined unit.	Remarks.
2nd Lt.	H.H.ALLEN.	17.4.18.	Wounded 28.5.18.Returned 18.6.1
2nd Lt.	H. DEMAINE.	18.6.18.	Awarded M.C. 18.11.18.
Lieut.	G.V.SCOTT.	23.7.18.	a/Capt. 23.7.18.
2nd Lt.	R.S.CAHN.	3.9.18.	
Lieut	D.R.LYNE.	13.11.18.	

98th FIELD COMPANY R.E.

Rank.	Name	Joined Unit	Remarks.
Major.	C.COFFIN.	2.11.14.	Transferred to H.Q.21st Div R.E. 1.6.15.
2/Lt.	N.AYRIS.	2.11.14.	Promoted T/Lt.11.7.15. Killed in action 31/12/15
2/Lt.	G.A.GREGSON.	28.11.14.	Promoted T/Lt.11.7.15. Wounded 15.12.15. Rejoined 2.1.16. Wounded 24.2.16. Rejoined 13.2.17. Wounded 16.6.17. Rejoined 10.8.17. Promoted A/Capt.17.8.17. Promoted T/Capt.13.9.17. Transferred to R.A.F. 17.7.18.
2/Lt.	H.TAYLOR.	11.12.14.	Promoted T/Lt.11.7.15. Killed in action 27.2.16.
2/Lt.	M.H.SCHWAB.	11.12.14.	Promoted T/Lt.11.7.15. to 104 Fd. Coy.R.E. 2nd in Command.
2/Lt.	G.E.LINES.	2.15.	To 126th Fd.Coy. 8.15.
Capt.	S.F.STOKES.	1.6.15.	Left Coy. about 13.8.15.
2/Lt.	A.W.METCALFE.	6.15.	Transferred to Newark 9.9.15.
Major	F.M.CLOSE.	22.6.15.	C.R.E. 14th Div.18.12.15.
Capt.	R.E.DEWING.	7.9.15.	Promoted A/Major on 18.12.15. to 17.1.16. Transferred to 223 Fd. Coy. 28.5.16.
Interpreter	R.M.G.BLONDEL.	9.9.18.	Transferred to H.Q R.E. 31.1.17. Awarded M.M. Nov 1916.
Capt.	H.J.COUCHMAN.	19.12.15.	Promoted A/Major 19.12.15. Awarded M.C. 3.6.16. Promoted Major 25.11.16. Appointed C.R.E. 39th Div. 1.7.17.
2/Lt.	J.W.BULL.	3.1.16.	Died of wounds 25.9.16.
2/Lt.	F.HEWIN.	18.2.16.	Wounded 3.10.17. Awarded M.C. 23.10.17. Mentioned in C. in C. Despatch 1.1.18. Promoted 30.11.16. to T/Lt.

98th Field Coy R.E. (continued).

Rank.	Name.	Joined Unit.	Remarks.
Lieut.	E.L.V.DAKIN.	2.3.16.	Appointed A/Capt.29.11.16. Appointed A/Major 2.7.17. Promoted T/Capt.18.9.17. Awarded M.C.22.10.17. Mentioned in C.in C. Despatch 111.18. Wounded & Missing 22.3.18.
2/ Lieut.	W.L.CAMPBELL.	4.6.16.	Promoted T/Lt 1.1.16 Transferred to 126th Field Coy.28.9.17. Rejoined Unit 3.6.18. Appointed A/Major. 2.6.18.
2/Lt.	W.P.F.McLAREN	29.6.16.	Appointed T/Lt. 2.1.18 Appointed A/Capt.17.7.18.
Lieut.	A.WILLIAMSON.	27.11.16.	Wounded at duty 5.10.17.
2/Lt.	G.HEPBURN.	13.12.16.	To 12th Fd.Coy.27.1.17.
2/Lt.	W.T.SHAVER.	28.5.17.	Killed in action 22.3.18.
2/Lt.	T.A.WOMERSLEY.	7.7.17.	Wounded 22.3.18. Awarded M.C. 4.5.18. Wounded 27.5.18. Promoted T/Lt. 25.9.18.
Lieut.	G.F.C.BAILE.	11.10.17.	Transferred to 126th Fd. Coy.14.10.17.
2/Lt.	T.H.McPHEE	14.12.17.	To Hospital 29.1.18.
2/Lt. *	G.BOOTES.	17.4.18.	To 97th Fd.Coy.20.4.18.
2/Lt.	R.L.CADELL.	17.4.18.	Wounded and Missing 28.5.18.
2/Lt.	H.La BOYD-MOSS	17.4.18.	Wounded 27.5.18.
2/Lt.	R.M.KAY.	17.4.18.	To Hospital 30.5.18
2/Lt.	L.W.LILLINGSTON	18.6.18.	Gassed 21.8.18.
2/Lt.	D.M.MENZIES.	18.6.18.	Awarded M.C. 24.9.18. Wounded at duty 26.10.18.
2/Lt.	E.F.MOLONY.	25.6.18.	Wounded 21.8.18. Rejoined 12.10.18.
2/Lt.	H.W.HILLIER.	5.7.18.	Wounded 22.3.18.
Lieut.	W.J.VAUGHAN-WILLIAMS.	16.7.18.	To 105th Coy. R.E. 3.8.18.
Lieut.	J.E.HARBEN.	27.7.18.	

98th Field Coy. R.E. (continued).

Rank.	Name.	Joined Unit.	Remarks.
2/Lt.	J.H. ST. JOHNSTON	28.8.18.	awarded M C 24.11.18
2/Lt.	W.H.CULLIS.	13.9.18.	To Hospital 15.10.18. Rejoined 1.11.18. To Hospital 2.11.18.
2/Lt.	F.H.G.STOCKDALE.	19.9.18.	Wounded 8.10.18.
Lieut.	D.R.LYNE. M.C.,	10.11.18.	To 97th Fd.Coy. 14.11.18.
* ~~Capt.~~ Lt.	A.H.SOUTAR. M.C.,	3.4.18.	Promoted A/Major 3.4.18. Wounded and Missing 28.5.18.

98th FIELD COMPANY R.E.

Rank.	Name	Joined Unit	Remarks.
Major.	C.COFFIN.	2.11.14.	Transferred to H.Q.21st Div R.E. 1.6.15.
2/Lt.	N.AYRIS.	2.11.14.	Promoted T/Lt.11.7.15. Killed in action 31/12/15
2/Lt.	G.A.GREGSON.	28.11.14.	Promoted T/Lt.11.7.15. Wounded 15.12.15. Rejoined 2.1.16. Wounded 24.2.16. Rejoined 13.2.17. Wounded 16.6.17. Rejoined 10.8.17. Promoted A/Capt.17.8.17. Promoted T/Capt.13.9.17. Transferred to R.A.F, 17.7.18.
2/Lt.	H.TAYLOR.	11.12.14.	Promoted T/Lt.11.7.15. Killed in action 27.2.16.
2/Lt.	M.H.SCHWAB.	11.12.14.	Promoted T/Lt.11.7.15. to 104 Fd. Coy.R.E.2nd in Command.
2/Lt.	G.E.LINES.	2.15.	To 126th Fd.Coy. 0.15.
Capt.	S.F.STOKES.	1.6.15.	Left Coy. about 13.8.15.
2/Lt.	A.W.METCALFE.	6.15.	Transferred to Newark 9.9.15.
Major	F.M.CLOSE.	22.6.15.	C.R.E. 14th Div.18.12.15.
Capt.	R.E.EWING.	7.9.15.	Promoted A/Major on 18.12.15. to 17.1.16. Transferred to 223 Fd. Coy. 28.5.16.
Interpreter	R.M.G.BLONDEL.	9.9.15.	Transferred to H.Q R.E. 31.1.17. Awarded M.M. Nov 1916
Capt.	H.J.COUCHMAN.	19.12.15.	Promoted A/Major 19.12.15. Awarded M.C. 3.6.16. Promoted Major 25.11.16. Appointed C.R.E. 39th Div. 1.7.17.
2/Lt.	J.W.BULL.	3.1.16.	Died of wounds 25.9.16.
2/Lt.	F.HEWIN.	18.2.16.	Wounded 3.10.17. Awarded M.C. 23.10.17. Mentioned in C. in C. Despatch 1.1.18. Promoted 30.11.16. to T/Lt.

98th Field Coy R.E. (continued).

Rank.	Name.	Joined Unit.	Remarks.
Lieut.	E.L.V.DAKIN.	2.3.16.	Appointed A/Capt.29.11.16. Appointed A/Major 2.7.17. Promoted T/Capt.18.9.17. Awarded M.C.22.10.17. Mentioned in C.in C. Despatch 1.11.18. Wounded & Missing 22.3.18.
[*T/*] Lieut.	W.L.CAMPBELL.	4.6.16.	[*Promoted T/Lt 1.1.16*] Transferred to 126th Field Coy.28.9.17. Rejoined Unit 3.6.18. Appointed A/Major. 2.6.18.
2/Lt.	W.P.F.McLAREN	29.6.16.	Appointed T/Lt. [*2.1.18*] Appointed A/Capt.17.7.18. Wounded at duty 5.10.17.
Lieut.	A.WILLIAMSON.	27.11.16.	To 12th Fd.Coy.27.1.17.
2/Lt.	G.HEPBURN.	13.12.16.	Killed in action 22.3.18.
2/Lt.	W.T.SHAVER.	28.5.17.	Wounded 22.3.18.
2/Lt.	T.A.WOMERSLEY.	7.7.17.	Awarded M.C. 4.5.18. Wounded 27.5.18. Promoted T/Lt. 25.9.18.
Lieut.	G.F.C.BAILE.	11.10.17.	Transferred to 126th Fd. Coy.14.10.17.
2/Lt. [*]	T.H.McPHEE	14.12.17.	To Hospital 29.1.18.
2/Lt.	G.BOOTES.	17.4.18.	To 97th Fd.Coy.20.4.18.
2/Lt.	R.L.CADELL.	17.4.18.	Wounded and Missing 28.5.18.
2/Lt.	H.La BOYD-MOSS	17.4.18.	Wounded 27.5.18.
2/Lt.	R.M.KAY.	17.4.18.	To Hospital 30.5.18
2/Lt.	L.W.LILLINGSTON	18.6.18.	Gassed 21.8.18.
2/Lt.	D.M.MENZIES.	18.6.18.	Awarded M.C. 24.9.18. Wounded at duty 26.10.18.
2/Lt.	E.F.MOLONY.	25.6.18.	Wounded 21.8.18. Rejoined 12.10.18.
2/Lt.	R.W.HILLIER.	5.7.18.	Wounded 22.3.18.
Lieut.	W.J.VAUGHAN-WILLIAMS.	16.7.18.	To 105th Coy. R.E. 3.8.18.
Lieut.	J.E.HARBEN.	27.7.18.	

98th Field Coy. R.E. (continued).

Rank.	Name.	Joined Unit.	Remarks.
2/Lt.	J.H. ST. JOHNSTON	28.8.18.	Awarded M.C. 24.11.18.
2/Lt.	W.H. CULLIS.	13.9.18.	To Hospital 15.10.18. Rejoined 1.11.18. To Hospital 2.11.18.
2/Lt.	F.H.G. STOCKDALE.	19.9.18.	Wounded 8.10.18.
Lieut.	D.R. LYNE. M.C.,	10.11.18.	To 97th Fd.Coy. 14.11.18.
* ~~Capt.~~ Lt.	A.H. SOUTAR. M.C.,	3.4.18.	Promoted A/Major 3.4.18. Wounded and Missing 28.5.18.

98th Field Coy R.E. (continued).

Rank.	Name.	Joined Unit.	Remarks.
Lieut.	E.L.V.DAKIN.	2.3.16.	Appointed A/Capt.29.11.16. Appointed A/Major 2.7.17. Promoted T/Capt.18.9.17. Awarded M.C.22.10.17. Mentioned in C.in C. Despatch 1.1.18. Wounded & Missing 22.3.18. Promoted T/Lt 1.1.16
2/Lieut.	W.L.CAMPBELL.	4.6.16.	Transferred to 126th Field Coy.28.9.17. Rejoined Unit 3.6.18. Appointed A/Major. 2.6.18.
2/Lt.	W.P.F.McLAREN	29.6.16.	Appointed T/Lt. 2.1.18 Appointed A/Capt.17.7.18. Wounded at duty 5.10.17.
Lieut.	A.WILLIAMSON.	27.11.16.	To 12th Fd.Coy.27.1.17.
2/Lt.	G.HEPBURN.	13.12.16.	Killed in action 22.3.18.
2/Lt.	W.T.SHAVER.	28.5.17.	Wounded 22.3.18.
2/Lt.	T.A.WOMERSLEY.	7.7.17.	Awarded M.C. 4.5.18. Wounded 27.5.18. Promoted T/Lt. 25.9.18.
Lieut.	G.F.C.BAILE.	11.10.17.	Transferred to 126th Fd. Coy.14.10.17.
2/Lt.	T.R.McPHEE	14.12.17.	To Hospital 29.1.18.
2/Lt. *	G.BOOTES.	17.4.18.	To 97th Fd.Coy.20.4.18.
2/Lt.	R.L.CADELL.	17.4.18.	Wounded and Missing 28.5.18.
2/Lt.	H.La BOYD-MOSS	17.4.18.	Wounded 27.5.18.
2/Lt.	R.M.KAY.	17.4.18.	To Hospital 30.5.18
2/Lt.	L.W.LILLINGSTON	18.6.18.	Gassed 21.8.18.
2/Lt.	D.M.MENZIES.	18.6.18.	Awarded M.C. 24.9.18. Wounded at duty 26.10.18.
2/Lt.	E.F.MOLONY.	25.6.18.	Wounded 21.8.18. Rejoined 12.10.18.
2/Lt.	H.W.HILLIER.	5.7.18.	Wounded 22.3.18.
Lieut.	W.J.VAUGHAN-WILLIAMS.	16.7.18.	To 105th Coy. R.E. 2.8.18.
Lieut.	J.E.HARBEN.	27.7.18.	

98th FIELD COMPANY R.E.

Rank.	Name	Joined Unit	Remarks.
Major.	C.COFFIN.	2.11.14.	Transferred to H.Q.21st Div R.E. 1.6.15.
2/Lt.	N.AYRIS.	2.11.14.	Promoted T/Lt.11.7.15. Killed in action 31/12/15
2/Lt.	G.A.GREGSON.	28.11.14.	Promoted T/Lt.11.7.15. Wounded 15.12.15. Rejoined 2.1.16. Wounded 24.2.16. Rejoined 13.2.17. Wounded 16.6.17. Rejoined 10.8.17. Promoted A/Capt.17.8.17. Promoted T/Capt.13.9.17. Transferred to R.A.F. 17.7.18.
2/Lt.	H.TAYLOR.	11.12.14.	Promoted T/Lt.11.7.15. Killed in action 27.2.16.
2/Lt.	M.H.SCHWAB.	11.12.14.	Promoted T/Lt.11.7.15. to 104 Fd. Coy.R.E.2nd in Command.
2/Lt.	G.E.LINES.	[illegible] 2.15.	To 126th Fd.Coy. 3.15.
Capt.	S.F.STOKES.	1.6.15.	Left Coy. about 13.8.15.
2/Lt.	A.W.METCALFE.	6.15.	Transferred to Newark 9.9.15.
Major	F.M.CLOSE.	22.6.15.	C.R.E. 14th Div.18.12.15.
Capt.	R.E.DEWING.	7.9.15.	Promoted A/Major on 18.12.15. to 17.1.16. Transferred to 223 Fd. Coy. 28.5.16.
Interpreter	R.M.G.BLONDEL.	9.9.18.	Transferred to H.Q R.E. 31.1.17. *Awarded M.M. Nov 1916*
Capt.	H.J.COUCHMAN.	19.12.15.	Promoted A/Major 19.12.15. Awarded M.C. 3.6.16. Promoted Major 25.11.16. Appointed C.R.E. 39th Div. 1.7.17.
2/Lt.	J.W.BULL.	3.1.16.	Died of wounds 25.9.16.
2/Lt.	F.HEWIN.	18.2.16.	Wounded 3.10.17. Awarded M.C. 23.10.17. Mentioned in C. in C. Despatch 1.1.18. Promoted 30.11.16. to T/Lt.

98th Field Coy. R.E. (continued).

Rank.	Name.	Joined Unit.	Remarks.
2/Lt.	J.H.ST.JOHNSTON	28.8.18.	Awarded M.C. 24.11.18
2/Lt.	W.H.CULLIS.	13.9.18.	To Hospital 15.10.18. Rejoined 1.11.18. To Hospital 2.11.18.
2/Lt.	F.H.G.STOCKDALE.	19.9.18.	Wounded 8.10.18.
Lieut.	D.R.LYNE. M.C.,	10.11.18.	To 97th Fd.Coy. 14.11.18.
* ~~Capt.~~ Lt.	A.H.SOUTAR. M.C.,	3.4.18.	Promoted A/Major 3.4.18. Wounded and Missing 28.5.18.

www.ingramcontent.com/pod-product-compliance
Lightning Source LLC
Chambersburg PA
CBHW081526160426
43191CB00011B/1690
* 9 7 8 1 4 7 4 5 1 1 9 9 5 *